Complete Guide
to the
Split-Pro Defense

GAILORD BELLAMY

PARKER PUBLISHING COMPANY, INC.   West Nyack, N. Y.

To my wife and children, Sharon, Kent, and Loraine, and to my parents, Ruth and Horace, for their love and understanding throughout the years.

PRINTED IN THE UNITED STATES OF AMERICA
ISBN 0-13-160606-9
BC

FOREWORD

I have known Gailord Bellamy as a head coach at South High School, Wichita, Kansas, as a graduate assistant here at Kansas State University, and in his present position as Assistant Head Football Coach at Central State College, Edmond, Oklahoma. When I learned that he was writing a book on defense for the well-known Parker series of coaching books, I was certain we'd end up with something extremely valuable because he has a knowledge of defensive football second to none and is one of the best-read coaches I know. Nevertheless, I wasn't quite prepared for as interesting and important a manuscript as I've just finished reading.

Coach Bellamy's book is timely, accurate, thorough, and comprehensive. It is well organized. Coach Bellamy first presents the whole defense. He then analyzes it in detail, position by position, and adds the coverages. Numerous, clear, and meaningful illustrations accompany each detailed step of explanation.

This means that the book deals with specifics, not with generalities. You probably couldn't get a "name" coach to reveal as much as is found in this book. But then there's little doubt in my mind that Coach Bellamy, already certainly one of the top small college defensive coaches, will be a "name" in the near future.

Vince Gibson

Head Football Coach
Kansas State University

WHAT THIS BOOK WILL SHOW YOU

This book illustrates in detail all aspects of the split defense and its variations. But the defensive system presented here is not limited solely to the split defense. Many defenses are included that will complement the split defense, evolving into a system of defenses that I call the Split-Pro.

The idea behind the Split-Pro defensive system is to "make things happen" and to "force the big play" by pressure and confusion tactics. The split defensive alignment is especially valuable in this respect because it is easily adjusted to stunting, dogging, and blitzing maneuvers.

The Split-Pro defensive system is presented in a systematic fashion so that any coach can easily install the complete system or any given part. The method of overall defensive organization and breakdown can easily be adapted to any defensive system on the college or high school level.

The first few chapters are devoted to individual player basics, the fundamentals, adjustments, stunts (individual, unit, group, and team) both up front and in the secondary. Also included are chapters containing basic team defenses, basic mixers, short yardage defenses, pass rushing defenses, pass defending defenses, prevent defenses, goal line defenses, automatics, and special tips on how to cope with special threats using defensive variations and stunts. In the concluding chapters, overall defensive organization and game strategy are covered.

In order to be flexible, attacking, defending, and yet simple, a special system of communications was devised for the Split-Pro. This system is simple and allows the type of play to be varied under actual game conditions. It also provides the defensive signal-caller with the tools to attack and to overload the offense in any area desired. This book explains the communications system in detail.

Throughout the book the reader will find many coaching points (C.P.) and illustrations of the correct and occasionally of the incorrect way of executing a specific technique or play. The reader will find these coaching points helpful and informative.

Gailord Bellamy

Acknowledgements

Like many other coaches, the author is a fanatic collector of concepts and ideas in all areas of football. As a result, very little was left unrecorded and unfiled over the years from the various sessions with a great many coaches from all over the country. Since the contributors are too numerous to list, the author wishes to acknowledge and express appreciation to those who have, in one way or another, helped to enrich the author's knowledge of the game of football and how to coach it.

Also, a special appreciation is herewith expressed to my college coaches: Jack Mitchell, George Bernhardt, Don Fambrough, Pete Tilman, and "Woody" Woodard for their help during my four years of college competition.

To Coach George Karras and Gary Wyant for their help while I was coaching on the high school level.

To Coach Vince Gibson and his staff at Kansas State University for the chance to coach, understudy, and observe the finer points of organizing, promoting, and developing a football program on the college level.

To Coach Chuck Fairbanks and his staff at Oklahoma University for their help and coaching suggestions.

To Central State College's Athletic Director Dale Hamilton and Head Football Coach Phil Ball for their permission to copy the game film clips that are included in this book. Without Coach Phil Ball's vote of confidence and delegated freedom to devise, install, and then test—under actual game conditions—many of the ideas included in this book would still be on the drawing board.

The author also wishes to thank Assistant Coaches Gary Howard and Val Reneau for their valuable encouragement and suggestions; and John Gumm, photographer, for his labors in developing and enlarging the photos used throughout the book.

Appreciation is also expressed to typists Marilyn Buchanan, Sally Teuscher, and Barbara Phillips for their labors and valuable suggestions.

CONTENTS

Foreword 5

What This Book Will Show You 7

Table of Abbreviations and Symbols Used In This Book 10

1. Evolution of the Split-Pro Defense 13

2. How to Coach Split-Pro Defensive End Techniques 27

3. How to Coach Split-Pro Strongside Linebacker
   Techniques (Sam) 49

4. How to Coach Split-Pro Inside Linebacker Techniques
   (Mike and Willie) 71

5. How to Coach Split-Pro Tackle Techniques
   (Right and Left) 107

6. How to Coach Weak Outside Linebacker Techniques
   (Rover) 125

7. How to Coach Split-Pro Secondary Pass Coverage Procedures
   and Techniques (Rover, Hounds and Fox) 135

8. How to Coach Split-Pro Secondary Team Coverages 155

9. How to Coach Split-Pro Secondary Stunts and Attacking
   Techniques 173

10. The Split-Pro Team Defenses 185

11. How to Use the "Split-Pro" Defensive System 199

    Index 220

9

TABLE OF ABBREVIATIONS AND SYMBOLS USED IN THIS BOOK

A. General Abbreviations:

    C.P.:   — Coaching points

    L.O.S. — Line of scrimmage

    SL   — Sideline

B. Defense:

    1. Letters

        R — Weak outside linebacker (Rover)

        E — Defensive end (right and left)

        T — Tackle (right and left)

        B — Linebacker (any)

        H — Defensive halfback (Hound)

        F — Defensive safety (Fox)

        M — Strong inside linebacker (Mike)

        W — Weak inside linebacker (Willie)

        S — Strong side linebacker (Sam)

    2. Symbols

        ⟶   Direction of movement

        - - - - - - -   Line of sight and key

        ⊢   Contact with offensive man

        〜〜〜〜   Cheating movement before snap

        [ ]   Area of diagram under discussion

        ⬭   Area of field covered by pass defender

        ◑   Darkened area indicates side that defensive man is favoring (Offensive linemen only)

C. Offense

   1. Letters

      QB — Quarterback
      SE — Split End
      FL — Flanker
      TE — Tight End
      HB — Halfback
      FB — Fullback
      TB — Tailback
      SB — Slotback
      WB — Wingback

   2. Symbols

Direction of movement

Block by offensive man; the extended mark indicates the side that the offensive blocker's head is on upon contact with the defender

A point at which a handoff of the ball is executed

Path of the ball in the air (can be pass or pitch)

Man in motion before the snap

Offensive man

Offensive center

Half-shaded circle of backfield men means that they handle the ball but transfer it to another back before it crosses the line of scrimmage

Final ball carrier

EVOLUTION OF
THE SPLIT-PRO DEFENSE

The system of defenses described in this book is an outgrowth of trial and error, college and professional film study, and the integration of notes recorded during sessions with coaches from all areas of the country on both the college and professional levels. As a result, the Split-Pro defensive system is a combination of ideas taken from many defensive systems of the past and present.

In developing the Split-Pro defensive system the author has strived to blend together some of the better features of the wide tackle-6 defense (in which the linebackers played over the offensive tackles and the tackles played over the ends), the Split-6 defense (or 6-2-3 in which the backers are over the center-guard seams), the Eagle defense (alignment popularized by Coach Greasy Neale in which the backers play over the offensive ends), the 5-4 monster defense (in which a player flip-flops from one side of the offensive formation to the other making that area stronger against the run or pass), the multi-stunting 4-4 (in which stunting possibilities are unlimited), and the Pro type 4-3 (which provides a balanced defensive alignment that is easily adjusted to overload against the run or pass).

As indicated by the title of this book, the two basic starting alignments are the "Split" and the "Pro." The combination of the "Split and "Pro" as basic defenses presents many interesting advantages.

The "Split" and the "Pro" defenses provide three basic needs. First, the "Split" provides an alignment that can overload and create blocking confusion for the running game. Second, the "Pro" alignment provides the ultimate in pass coverage. And third, a mixture of the two is easily obtained since the type of personnel needed and the techniques to be taught are very similar in most respects.

As far as the "Split" alignment is concerned, it is not radically new, and has been used sparingly by a few coaches on all levels, in one form or the other for some time. It is only recently that the alignment has gained the interest of coaches all across the nation. Some of the more obvious reasons for the added interest is the result of new and effective developments and the success it is achieving in major college circles. Certainly the success of Notre Dame and Penn State in recent years with this particular type of alignment has served to develop additional interest.

The Split defense (sometimes referred to as the Inside 4-4, the Split-6, Split-4, Notre Dame 4-4, or Penn State 4-4) is a fascinating defense to work with. Its popularity will continue to grow on both the college and high school levels, and rightfully so, for the alignment has enough possibilities that it may very well become the next national defense.

Since the Split defense discussed in this book is blended with ideas taken from other defenses of the past and present, a general understanding is necessary before the specifics of the defense are discussed.

A. Start of the Split-Pro Defensive System.
   1. Background
      The Split-Pro Defensive System is composed of the best features of the wide tackle-6, split-6, 5-4 monster, 4-4, Eagle, and the Pro type 4-3.
      "Split" refers to the basic alignment, while "Pro" refers to a variation of the split defense that strengthens the pass coverage. Pro in this system does resemble a true 4-3 type alignment; however, it is altered in some respects.
      As stated before, the split defense is composed of ideas taken from various defensive systems. For example:
      a. The split principle was taken from the split-6 defense that aligned two linebackers in the middle between the two guards. (See Figures 1 and 2)

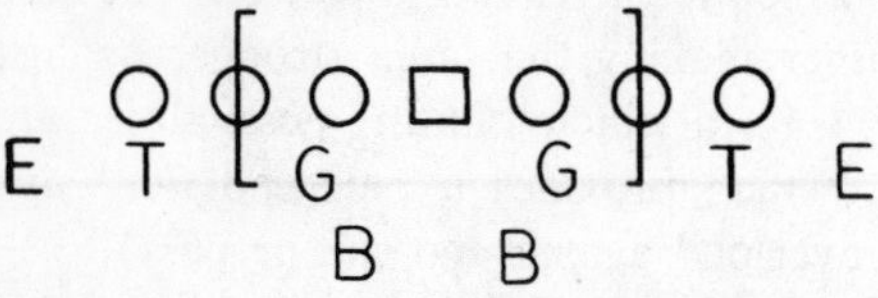

Figure 1 Split-6 Backer Alignment

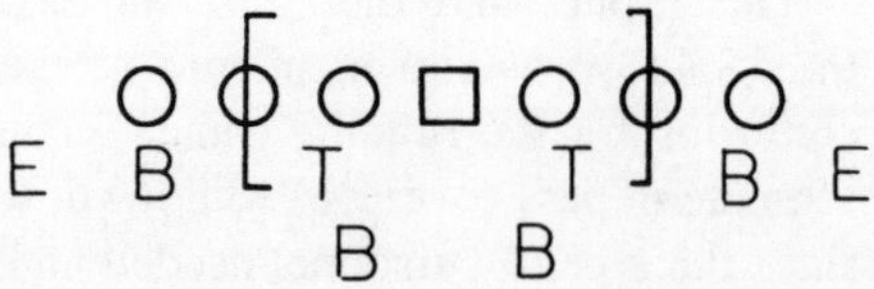

Figure 2 The New Split Alignment

b. In the new split defense the backers will scrape toward flow presenting the offensive line with wide tackle-6 blocking problems. (See Figures 3 and 4a and b)

Figure 3 Wide Tackle-6

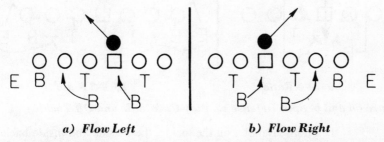

a) Flow Left   b) Flow Right

Figure 4a and b How the Wide Tackle-6 Alignment Is Obtained After Flow Begins

c. In order to aid the secondary, secure the off-tackle hole, discourage the outside running and sprint out attack. The inside eye alignment on the tight ends was also included in the basic Split defense. This position keeps the end from blocking down on the inside backers, holds him up as a receiver, and strengthens the flank. (See Figure 5a and b)

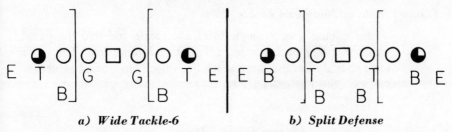

a) Wide Tackle-6   b) Split Defense

Figure 5a and b Outside Personnel Alignment in Wide Tackle-6 and Split Defenses

d. As far as the ends are concerned, they are turned loose to play true end techniques. They are free to rush and contain. They have no pass coverage responsibilities involving cushion, slow rotation, or otherwise.

2. How the Split Defense Creates Blocking Problems

The reason why the split defensive alignment is difficult to run against is that there are four defenders against three linemen at the point of attack. (Lead blocks by backs, as well as fold blocks by guards and traps will be discussed later in this chapter.)

If a play threatens the middle, the tackles squeeze and the backers plug, making a ratio of four to three from guard to guard. If a play threatens off-tackle, the ratio is still four to three. (See Figure 6a and b)

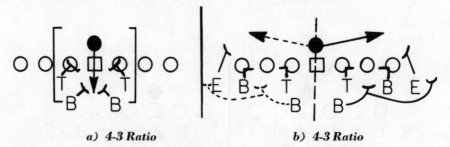

a) 4-3 Ratio   *b) 4-3 Ratio*

Figure 6a and b Split Defense vs. Play Up-Middle and Off-Tackle

If the offense doubles on the tackle, the outside and inside backers come free. (See Figure 7)

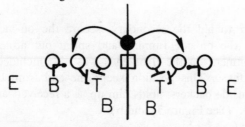

Figure 7 Split vs. Double on Tackle

If the offense tries to single block the tackle and fold the guard around on either backer, one backer should come free. The other backer should meet the guard at the line of scrimmage and neutralize his block. (See Figure 8a and b)

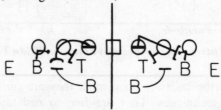

a) Outside Backer Free   *b) Inside Backer Free*

Figure 8a and b Split vs. Fold and Cross Back

If the offense sends the offensive tackle on the inside backer, the defensive tackle (keeping gap arm free) should slide into the hole along with the outside backer. (See Figure 9)

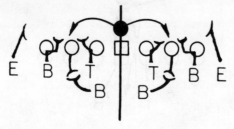

Figure 9 Split vs. Tackle on Inside Backer

If the offense attempts to bounce the offensive tackle off the defensive tackle, and then pick up the inside backer, it is too slow to be an effective block on the backer. (See Figure 10) Also, the outside backer is again free.

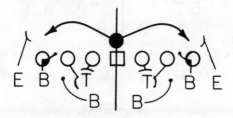

Figure 10 Split vs. "Tackle Bounce" Block

If the offense uses a reach block to get outside, the backer and the end come free because the center, end and tackle should not be able to get to the backer or end fast enough. (See Figure 11)

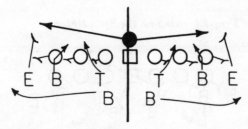

Figure 11 Split vs. Reach Blocking

When the offense attempts to run outside they must contend with free-end play and cut off a linebacker who is usually free of line blocks from end to end.

In order to run effectively against the split alignment, the offense is forced to lead block with the backs, fold with the guards, and cross, or trap block with the guards or tackles. (See Figures 12, 13a and b, 14, and 15)

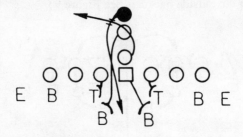

Figure 12 Lead Block by Backs vs. the Split Defense

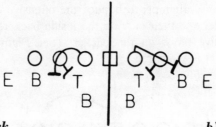

a) The Fold Block   *b) The Cross Block*

Figure 13a and b Fold and Cross Blocks by Guards vs. the Split Defense

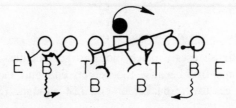

Figure 14 Tackle Trap Blocking vs. the Split Defense

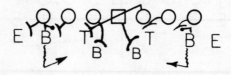

Figure 15 Guard Trap Blocking vs. the Split Defense

When the offense resorts to crossing, trapping, and fold-blocking, the split stunts are even more effective. Counter traps are the only plays that should cause real problems. However, daily drill on tackle squeeze and inside backer reads should help alleviate this problem.

If the offense chooses to throw the ball, they must contend with hard rushing ends, various stunts, and secondary coverages that shift from tough man to loose defending zone.

Some of the more important aspects of the Split Defense are:

1. It provides a four man rush on the side of flow, causing problems for the sprint out and sweeps.
2. The split alignment with various stunts causes blocking confusion for the offensive line.
3. The alignment affords many dogging and blitzing possibilities making it tough to get consistent protection for the quarterback.
4. A variety of coverages involving man-to-man, zone, roll zone, combination zone and man, along with bump-and-go tactics, make it hard for the quarterback to read the coverages.
5. Flexible communications make the defense easy to adjust under actual game conditions. This is especially valuable for stopping a consistent running or pass play.

3. Developing the Split-Pro Defensive System
   a. Separate Units

   As some coaches have divided the 4-4, the Split defense was divided into various small groups for stunting purposes and simple communications. The Split defense is divided into five units: (a) an end and outside backer unit, (b) a tackle unit, (c) an inside backer unit, (d) another end and outside backer unit, and (e) a secondary unit. (See Figure 16a, b, c, d, and e)

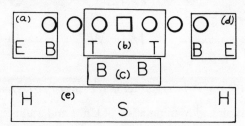

Figure 16a, b, c, d, and e   Breakdown of Defense by Units

The designation and manipulation of the five units (separately and coordinately) will be taken up in complete detail in a later section.

   b. Identification of Personnel

   To improve communication, the players are assigned names or letters:

RE, LE — Stand for ends, right and left.

S   — Stands for "Sam." Sam goes to the strong side of the formation over the tight end. Sam is also classified as the strong outside linebacker.

RT, LT — Stand for tackles, right and left.

M   — Stands for "Mike." Mike is the signal caller and will align on the strong side of the formation. He is classified as the strong inside linebacker.

W   — Stands for "Willie." Willie is the weak inside linebacker.

R   — Stands for "Rover." Rover will align on either side of the formation and will declare much like a monster. The side he aligns on is determined by the defense called, scouting report, field position, or down and distance.

H   — Stands for the halfbacks (Hounds). The halfbacks may or may not change sides, depending upon personnel and scouting report.

F   — Stands for the safety (Fox). The safety calls the secondary coverages and controls the play of the halfbacks.

Figure 17 illustrates the Split alignment and identification of personnel.

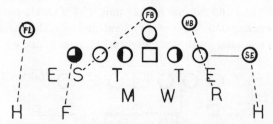

Figure 17 Identification of Personnel in the Split-Pro Defense

c. Designation and Manipulation of Units and Stunts

As stated before, the front people (8) are divided into four pairs, each called a unit. Each unit (for stunting purposes) is identified as follows:

Sam Unit   — Consists of Sam and end on his side.
Tackle Unit — Consists of both right and left tackles.
Backer Unit — Consists of both inside backers, Mike and Willie.
Rover Unit — Consists of Rover and end on his side.

The stunts are also divided into four categories: individual, unit, group, and team. Individual stunts are those involving only one player (can be any one player named). Unit stunts involve two players (Sam unit, tackle unit, backer unit, or Rover unit). The group stunts involve two units stunting together at one time (Sam and Rover or tackles and backers).

If more than two groups are stunting at one time it is called a team stunt. (See Figure 18a, b, c, and d)

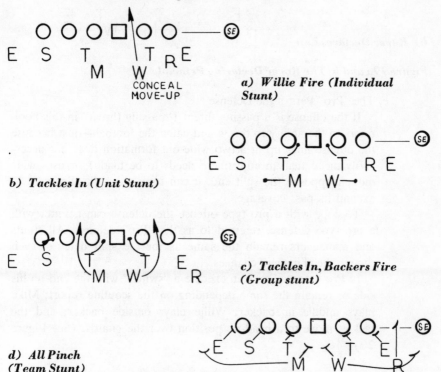

a) *Willie Fire (Individual Stunt)*

b) *Tackles In (Unit Stunt)*

c) *Tackles In, Backers Fire (Group stunt)*

d) *All Pinch (Team Stunt)*

Figure 18a, b, c, and d Designation and Manipulation of Stunts

d. Flip-flopping Personnel

The monster principle is also used with the split-pro defensive system; this man in the split-pro defense is referred to as the "Rover." Similar to the monster in most defensive systems, the Rover can declare to either side of the offensive formation. Sam, the strong outside linebacker, will also change from side to side in order to align on the tight end. Sam will do this regardless of which side the Rover declares. Therefore, it is possible to have both players on the same side. (See Figure 19 a and b)

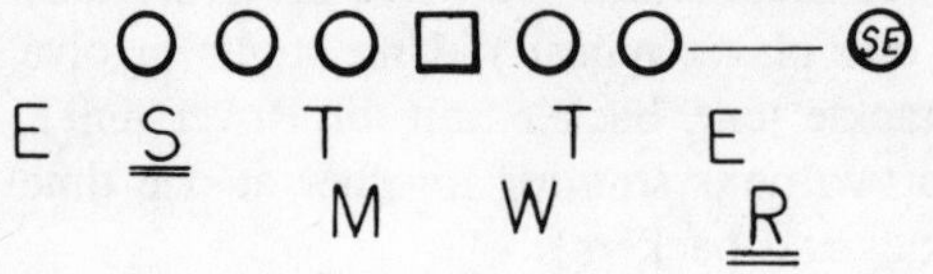

○ ○ ○ □ ○ ○ —— ⓈⒺ
E S̲ T   T   E
      M   W   R̲   *a) Rover Declares Right*

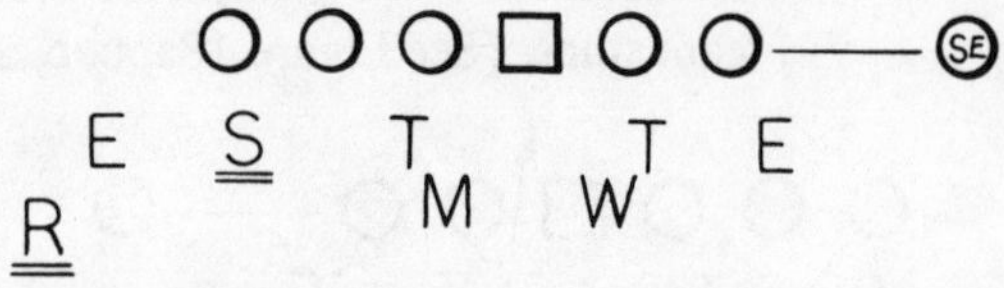

○ ○ ○ □ ○ ○ —— ⓈⒺ
E S̲ T   E
b) Rover Declares Left   R̲   M   W

Figure 19a and b The Rover Declaring Principle

e. The "Pro" Part of the Defense

If the offense is a passing threat ("passing threat" in this book refers to the ability to throw and catch the football—just because the offense lines up in a two wide-out formation does not necessarily mean that an adjustment needs to be made) or uses wide motion opposite the split end, it can force the split alignment to expand its pass coverage.

To cope with a pro type offense the defense can counter with a pro type defense, referred to as the "Pro" defense. All stunts and maneuvers remain the same as for the split defense, even though the alignment changes.

In Pro defense Sam can execute a "switch" with the end on his side or remain the same depending on the scouting report; Mike plays middle linebacker; Willie plays outside backer; and the tackles move to a head-up position over the guards. (See Figure 20)

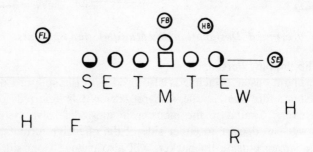

Figure 20 Pro Defense

B. The Basic Defenses
   1. A Quick Glance at the Split-Pro Defenses

The Split-Pro defensive system actually provides three types of play. The Split alignment provides the best alignment to pressure from, the Pro alignment provides the best alignment to defend from, and the blended mixture of the two provides the balance between pressure and defense.

The tempo of play can also be regulated in both the Split and Pro alignments. From either alignment two basic types of play are used. They are called "Go" and "Read." These two calls regulate the tempo of play involving the tackle and backer units.

In Split or Pro "Go," the tackles and inside backers attack the offensive linemen forcing play with all-out aggressiveness and speed. In Split or Pro "Read," the tackles and inside backers read, hit, control, react, and then pursue. Figures 21a and b illustrate the two alignments while 22a and b illustrate the two types of play.

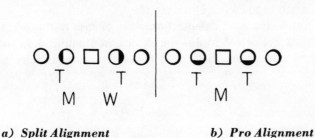

a) Split Alignment   *b) Pro Alignment*

Figure 21a and b   Split and Pro Alignments

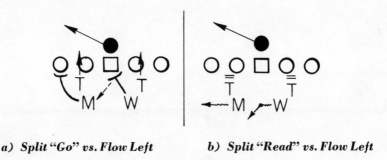

a) Split "Go" vs. Flow Left   *b) Split "Read" vs. Flow Left*

Figure 22a and b   Split "Go" and "Read" Techniques

Summary

Basically, the "Split" and "Pro" are the major defenses. The Split defense is stronger vs. the running game while the Pro defense provides more security in the secondary. By using a mixture of the two, most problems created by the offense can be coped with easily.

At this point it may be well to enumerate the advantages of the Split defense and the Pro defense. The chapters to follow will cover in detail the approach to using this defensive system. It is felt that the coach derives the following advantages by using the Split defense:

1. Good free end play—gives the option, sprint out, and sweeps a problem.
2. Provides a better drop back pass rush and backside rush vs. the sprint out.
3. Takes less versatile ends—they do not have pass coverage responsibilities.
4. Provides a good alignment to stunt from.
5. Spacing and alignment creates blocking confusion—the offense must lead, fold, and trap block.
6. The split alignment is easily adjusted to various other alignments.
7. The attacking techniques will force offensive play, "making things happen" and creating "the big play."
8. Overall, the Split defense forces the offense to do things that they would prefer not to do—block against stunting defenses, work in long yardage situations, and throw the football under pressure.

2 HOW TO COACH SPLIT-PRO DEFENSIVE END TECHNIQUES

General comment

The qualifications of the ends in the Split-Pro defensive system differ slightly from other defenses due to their assigned responsibilities. The ends should be large and strong enough to contain the power sweeps from a true end position. Occasionally, the ends are asked to play a "down" (3 or 4 point position on the L. O. S.) position on the outside shoulder of the offensive tackles (the "switched" position) in the "Pro" defense.

The ends' responsibilities are to contain outside plays, rush the passer and trail if flow is away. The ends are not involved in pass coverage, a cushion, or a slow rotation when flow is away as required in some of the current defensive systems. This "free" type of end play requires less teaching time, allows a less versatile individual to play the position, and requires less thinking on the part of the player. Therefore, the ends can play the running and passing game with all-out enthusiasm and aggressiveness.

A. Concept: In the split defense the ends will usually put on the hard rush. The defensive ends are not responsible for pass coverage or rotation out the backside when flow is away.

B. Special Calls

The ends listen for assignment calls from Sam or Rover (whichever is on their side and play accordingly).

    1. The "Me" call—the end plays tough inside and off-tackle, he does not have to contain the outside plays, the linebackers will do this.

    2. The "You" call—End must contain all outside plays. The linebackers will fill inside.

3. The "Gone" call—End contains same as for a "You" call. End has no immediate help inside or outside from Sam or Rover backer.

4. "No call"—End plays true end techniques and contains or trails as needed. End has no immediate help inside or outside from the Sam or Rover backer.

C. Stance: (A two point stance). The end should align 1-1½ yards outside the end man on the line of scrimmage with the body bent at the knees (not at the waist) and the shoulders square to the line of scrimmage. The inside foot should be forward and the outside foot back.

D. Focal Point: The end keys the near back's outside shoulder for initial reaction (No halfback key fullback). After the snap, the end analyzes the backfield action and line play (pulling linemen). (See Figure 23)

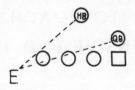

Figure 23 The Ends Focal Points

Ends, Don Eldridge #88 and Richard Dixon #85 in the "Split Defense" alignment. Notice their positions; Dixon is using the basic stance while Eldridge is using the "Box" stance because of a potential crack back blocker. (Central State vs. Northeastern)

E. Initial Move: 1) The end reacts on the snap by shuffling and reading the
   near back. 2) During the shuffle, the end should aim at the outside hip
   of the near back; no near back, then penetrate to a point two yards deep.
F. End Keys and Techniques:

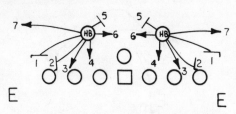

Figure 24 The Ends Keys and Seven Initial Moves

#1—Hook: a) Blocker Low—Jam outside hand into helmet and inside
   hand on shoulder pad—do not let him hook you; work to the outside and contain. b) Blocker High—Meet with inside shoulder forearm lift, neutralize him, and play off the block to contain.
#2—Kick Out: Meet with inside shoulder forearm lift—(bring it up from
   the inside knee) squeeze the play down. Be in position to fall off
   outside if runner swings back and deep. Work laterally down the
   line of scrimmage. Do not turn shoulder inside. Meet the block in
   good position.
#3—Belly or Lead: Look for guard kick-out or turn-out block. (Meet
   with inside shoulder forearm lift.) Squeeze play inside.
#4—Dive and Option: Look for guard kick-out or tackle kick-out.
   Squeeze the play. If option, take Pitch man, work laterally and make
   quarterback keep the ball, but do not run out too quickly—get inside hand up and in face of the quarterback. Point at pitch man
   with other hand keeping both of the backs in view. Shuffle down
   the line of scrimmage with shoulders square, making the quarterback keep the ball. (See Figure 25)

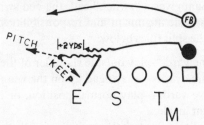

Figure 25 The Ends Techniques for Playing the Option

#5—Pass Protects: Rush the passer using various pass rush techniques.
   (See rushing the passer.) Never hit solidly, must also contain.
#6—Pitch and Quick Outside Plays: Contain and force plays deep—

make them belly back. If you lose containment, take a post route to pursue. Do not chase ball carrier to sideline from behind; get the angle unless you know for sure that you can catch him. (See Figure 26)

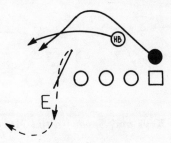

Figure 26 End Force and Contain Angle

C.P.: If ends lose contain they should cushion back through at correct intercepting angle.

#7—Flow Away: Trail, move flat at first looking for counter trap. (Look for trapper.) Then, get depth even with deepest back. When reverse threat is gone, take a far post route in pursuit. (Angle depends on lateral field position) (See Figure 27)

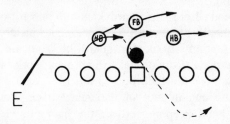

Figure 27 End's Trail and Pursuit Angles

G. Split Rules: If Sam gives a "switch" call, the end switches positions with him. (See Sam's basic alignment and responsibilities.) If no switch call, the end applies the split rules below.

  1. Wing split one yard—play outside shoulder of the wing man.
  2. Wing split three yards—play head up on the wing man.
  3. Wing split five yards—play normal position, or line up head on the wing and stunt inside.
  4. Against a split end—switch positions with the first inside linebacker.

H. The "Switch" Call: The end and outside linebacker (Sam or Rover) combination may set regular (end outside) or switch (linebacker outside). This decision is made by Sam or Rover shortly after the offense breaks the huddle. (See Sam Split Rules)

Figure 28 The Sam and Rover "Switch"

1. The ends "switch" position vs. a split end: the split side end uses the same stance (2 point) or down in a three point stance. He lines up on the outside eye or shoulder of the offensive tackle and takes a short step with inside foot to neutralize the tackle. The key is through the near back, looking for the lead and trap blocks. Objective—close the off-tackle hole.
2. The ends "switch" position vs. a close slot: the end lines up head-on with the slot back and steps to the slot with the outside foot mentally prepared to meet his block or a double team from him and the end. The end looks to the inside during the charge and must not be caved in or turned out.

I. The Ends "Loose" Call:

1. Purpose: Used as a prevent or long yardage situation alignment.
2. Reasoning: The advantages are that the end's vision is broader and he can "read" more players. The loose alignment gives the end more time "to read" and "to react" before blockers get to him. He can also support inside and outside better.
3. Stance: Normal but loosened up and turned slightly inside (45 degrees). Position depends on split of flanker or split end.
4. Technique: Read the play and react accordingly.

J. The Ends "Box" Call:

1. Purpose: Eliminates the crack block by outside men.
2. Stance: Face inside 2-2½ yards from last man on the line of scrimmage.
3. Technique: Box and contain.

K. Pro Defense Alignment
   In "split" defense and on a "check pro" call the ends line up 2-2½ yards outside the end man on the line of scrimmage. In "Pro" defense the alignment changes.
   a. Ends Alignment on "Pro" Defense.
      1. Stance: Automatic switch with the outside backer. End goes to a three point stance, with the inside foot forward and even with the outside foot of the offensive tackle.
      2. Technique: On movement (snap) the end drives the outside foot up, reacting to the block. If no contact he closes for the trap. (See Figure 29)

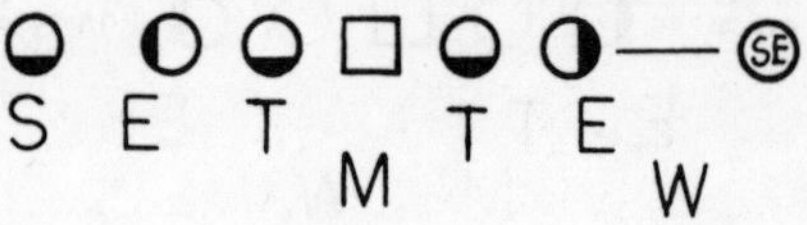

O O O O □ O O —— ⑤Ⓔ

S E T   T E
      M   W

Figure 29 The Ends "Pro" Alignment

b. Ends' Techniques on "Pro" Defense
  1. If the tackle blocks out on end:

    a) Use a one step attack, bringing the outside foot parallel at
       the snap.

    b) Neutralize and attack the man with a forearm shoulder lift.

    c) Fight through the man; do not circle his block.

    d) If he "hangs tough" with you, keep the feet moving. (See
       Figure 30)

Figure 30 Ends' First Step, "Pro" Alignment

2. If the Tight End Blocks Down:

    a) Take the first step.

    b) Step at the end with the outside foot on second step.

    c) Fight through the end's block.

3. End's Reaction to Cross Blocks:

    a) Take the first step.

    b) Step at guard with inside foot on second step.

    c) Neutralize the guard with an inside shoulder forearm lift.

    d) Do not turn inside and face the trapper. Keep the shoulders
      square with the line of scrimmage.

C.P.: Keep shoulders square to the line of scrimmage, close down the
hole and force the ball carrier inside to the linebackers.

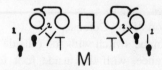

Figure 31 End's Steps vs. Cross Block

4. Ends Reaction to a Double Team Block:

a) Take the first step.
b) React to the drive blocker (take a dive). Fight through him (his inside knee, build a pile).

C.P.: Do not spin out and wall-off the Mike backer.

Figure 32 Correct Way of Fighting the Double Team Block

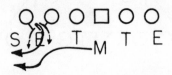

Figure 33 Incorrect Way of Fighting the Double Team (Spin Out). Backer has to give ground in order to get around the pile.

L. Rushing the Passer.
1. General Concept
The theory of the split defense is to "make things happen," and and "force the big play." If this happens and the running game is stymied, the offense will face many long yardage situations. Therefore, good pass rushing techniques are a must.

The defensive ends must put pressure on the passer. In order to do this they must develop an aggressive attitude and be fierce competitors vs. the pass. This is extremely important because much of the time the secondary will be in man-to-man coverage.

2. The Ends' Pass Rush Techniques
One of the most important aspects of rushing the passer is to keep progressing toward the passer while executing the techniques. The ends' normal rush lane will be with outside leverage keeping the quarterback in the pocket for the ·wolf pack (inside rushers). There will be times when the ends can rush inside forcing the quarterback out of the pocket—this will depend on the scouting report and the defensive design. On sure passing situations, the ends can eliminate the shuffle technique and fire directly in on the quarterback.

NOTE: Techniques Used Depend on Scout Report.

a. The Outside shoulder drive (Normal rush): Blast into outside shoulder of blocker (keep shoulder under his), defeat his block.

This is an all-out effort to physically over-power the blocker. It is extremely important that the ends master this technique because it baits the blocker for subsequent moves.

C. P.: 1) Over-power blocker—no fakes.
2) Shrink the pocket by forcing the blocker back and into the quarterback's lap.
3) Once this technique is successful, the blocker is set up for subsequent moves.

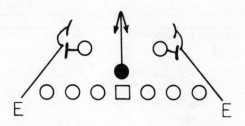

Figure 34 Outside Shoulder Drive—Normal Rush Technique

b. The Inside fake: Fake inside; when back sets up, go outside. (See Figure 35)

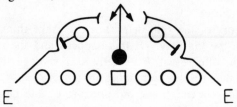

Figure 35 The Inside Fake

c. The Limp Leg: Good against the chop (low block) blocker. Give him a limp leg, pull him by, rush the passer with hands high.
d. The Butt and Go: Butt the blocker right in the chin—as he braces himself, grab his jersey and arms just below and behind the shoulder pads. Throw off and rush the passer with hands high.
e. The Outside Shoulder Drive and Inside Roll: Start the shoulder drive, bounce and roll inside, rushing the passer with hands high. (See Figure 36)

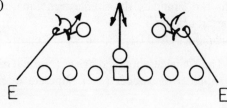

Figure 36 The Outside shoulder drive and inside roll

f. The Fake and Club: Fake one way or the other, as back moves to counter, club him on his way. Rush the passer with hands high.

g. The Hand Blow and Club: Drive at blocker delivering a hand blow into blocker's chin, helmet or chest, almost at the same time come across with the other hand into the helmet with a club.

3. Coaching Points (In sequence)

The ends should gun for the passer by squeezing his area of operation, forcing him into another rusher or out of his pocket. Make the quarterback throw on the run. If he throws, make him limit his choice of receivers to the first; do not give him time to find the second, force him to run. He may be a poor runner or dislike the contact (depends on scout report).

Key the depth of the quarterback. If he gets deeper than seven yards, look for a screen. When he sets up, and gets his hands up to throw, the ends should extend their hands vertically. The goal of the ends is to cut the vision of the quarterback in 2.9 seconds; get his attention, knock down the ball, tip the ball, force elevation of the throw, or force a bad throw. This in turn gives the secondary more time to get under the ball or cover more ground before the interception or reception.

M. The Ends' Stunts

All stunts are divided into four categories: individual, unit, group, and team. Individual stunts are those involving only one player. Unit stunts involve two players, the two tackles, the two inside linebackers, or the outside backer and the onside end. The group stunts involve two units working together. For example, if the inside backers and the tackles work a stunt it would be called a "group stunt." If more than two groups are stunting at the same time it is called a "team stunt."

1. Individual End Stunts

a) General Concept: There are times that another type of end play is needed to cope with special situations. Variations are obtained by individual end stunts.

b) The End's "Zip" Stunt

1) Stance: Regular or three point sprinters' stance. (Can be one or the other.)

2) Stunt: On movement (snap) crash recklessly, eliminating the shuffle. This stunt gives the end some freedom in choosing his own route.

    c) The Ends "Hold" Stunt
       1) Stance: Regular
       2) Stunt: On movement (snap) hold your ground, keying the play action. Wait and see what the offense is going to do before you cross the line of scrimmage.

2. Unit End Stunts
    a) General Concept: Sam, Rover, or the defensive signal-caller can call the unit stunts. The calls will tell the ends what they do— Sam and Rover do the opposite.
    b) The Two Units
       1) The Sam Unit—Includes Sam and the end on his side.
       2) The Rover Unit—Includes the Rover and the end on his side.

      These calls work the same, regardless of which side the Rover or Sam aligns. Stunt is called by designating which unit is to go —Sam or Rover. (See Figures 37-40)

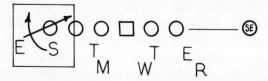

Figure 37 The "Sam In" Stunt

Figure 38 The "Rover In" Stunt

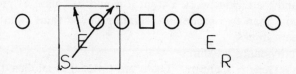

Figure 39 The "Sam Out" Stunt (Not Used vs. Tight End)

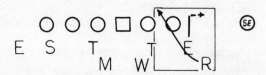

Figure 40 The "Rover Out" Stunt (Not Used vs. Tight End)

SPLIT DEFENSE -"SAM IN" STUNT

60 WEIGL (SAM)

85 DIXON (END)

1

(1) Sam (Chuck Weigl #60) and End (Richard Dixon #85) in the Split alignment ready to execute the "In" stunt.

BALL CARRIER

"END" CRASHES INSIDE

2

"SAM" LOOPS & CONTAINS

(2) At the snap the End crashes hard inside and Sam loops outside to contain.

(3) *After initial steps the End and Sam recognize the play and adjust accordingly. Notice the Tight End blocking out on Sam—this frees the End.*

(4) *End making the tackle on the Tailback at the line of scrimmage. (Central State vs. East Central)*

c) The "In" Stunt
1) Stance: Regular
2) Stunt: On the movement (snap) drive hard through a point where the outside hip of last man on the line of scrimmage would be. Take on all comers. If quarterback comes your way, take him. On the belly option take on the fullback and knock him into the quarterback, forcing the quarterback deeper and outside.

No Contain Responsibilities—If play gets outside, bow it up field and pursue the football. If ball goes away, trail. Sprint out to your side, get to the quarterback the best way you know how.

Dropback—free rush on quarterback. Inside or outside of backs' block no contain responsibilities. (See Figures 41 and 42)

Figure 41 The "Sam In" Stunt

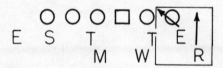

Figure 42 The "Rover In" Stunt

3) Purpose of the "In" Stunt—Fouls up close wing and slot blocking combinations. Destroys the option.
d) The "In Back" Stunt: End goes behind Sam and hits gap just inside of the last man on the line of scrimmage.
1) Stance: Same, but loosen slightly and may even cheat to assignment.
2) Stunt: Come off the line and behind Sam. End must get to a point where he can stop the dive play or anything off-tackle. Flow outside, work up field and down the line; flow away trail, drop back pass—rush the passer. (See Figure 43)

Figure 43 The "In Back" Stunt

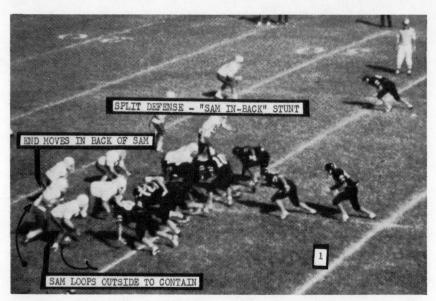

SPLIT DEFENSE - "SAM IN-BACK" STUNT

END MOVES IN BACK OF SAM

SAM LOOPS OUTSIDE TO CONTAIN

1

(1) Chuck Weigl #60 and Richard Dixon #85 starting the "In-Back" stunt. At the snap the End moves in back of Sam while Sam loops outside to contain.

BALL CARRIER

SAM & END READ PLAY & ADJUST

2

(2) After the initial steps the End and Sam recognize the play and adjust accordingly.

40

(3) *When the Tight End releases down field to get into the blocking lane no one is in position to block on the End.*

(4) *Since no one can block on the End he makes the tackle at the line of scrimmage. (Central State vs. East Central)*

3) Purpose of the "In Back" Stunt: Fouls up close wing and slot blocking combinations. Good vs. drop back protection.

e) The "Out" Stunt: Used on split end side.

   1) Stance: Regular

   2) Stunt: End has outside containment. Key near back through the tackle

Figure 44 The "Sam and Rover Out" Stunt

3. The Group End Stunts

  a) General Concept

    Group stunts will go by the same names and require the same techniques as the unit stunts. The only difference between unit stunts and group stunts is that more than one unit is stunting at the same time. Example: "Sam and Rover In" Stunt (See Figure 45)

Figure 45 The "Sam and Rover In" stunt

4. End Team Stunts

  a) "Blast" Stunts

    The blast stunt is an all-out effort by one side of the line. The other side of the line plays regular defense. The Ends' "Blast" Rules: If the stunt is called on your side—crash.

    If the stunt is called on the other side—play regular.

    1) The "Blast Right" Stunt. (See Figure 46)

Figure 46 The "Blast Right" Stunt

2) The "Blast Left" Stunt. (See Figure 47)

Figure 47 The "Blast Left" Stunt

b) The "Dog" Stunts
   1) General Concept
      A "Dog" (in this book) refers to an all-out six man rush. However, it is not always the same six. Rushers can come from all angles (see "Dogs" and pass rushes).
      The three deep secondary men cover man-to-man on the receivers; the names or assigned numbers of two other players are called to cover the two remaining backs should they release.
      If the opponents use more than one offensive formation or backfield set, as most teams do, the defensive signal caller may have to use an automatic call at the line of scrimmage. The backfield may shift from one set to another, so an automatic system for calling the dogs and blitzes is a must if maximum results are expected. The above remains true for the blitz stunts also.
   2) At the Line Automatics for the Dog and Blitz Stunts
      In order to effectively automatic to any of the dogs at the line of scrimmage, each possible pass defender is given a number. If the defender's number is called, he will cover the first back releasing on his side. If his number is not called, he is free to rush.
      With this system, all the signal caller has to do is make a huddle call of "dog" (or "blitz") and then make a two digit number (or one for a blitz) call at the line of scrimmage to match the offensive set.
   3) Number Assignments for Dogs and Blitzes
      Numbers are assigned to the eligible pass defenders, from left to right. The left defensive end is number one, the Sam linebacker is number two, the Mike linebacker is number three, the Willie linebacker is number four, the right end is number five, and the Rover linebacker is number six.
   4) The "15-Dog" (Ends' Dog) Stunt. The three deep secondary

will play man. The ends' numbers are called so they will cover the backs out if they release. (See Figure 48)

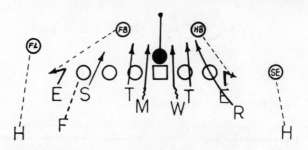

Figure 48 The "15-Dog" (Ends' Dog) Stunt

C.P.: On the "15-Dog" stunt the ends should key the tight end. If the tight end releases, shift key to the onside back; if he blocks, hang or rush as needed—watch hot route. If the tight end blocks on Sam, contain and play football. On all other "Dogs" the ends rush the passer with all-out effort.

     5) Other types of "Dogs" that can be used are 26-Dog (Sam and Rover), 24-Dog (Sam and Willie), 36-Dog (Mike and Rover), 16-Dog (End and Rover), and other obvious combinations of the six numbers. (Refer to pressure team stunts.)

  c. The "Blitz" Stunts (Seven man rushes)

    1) General Concept.

       A blitz refers to an all-out, seven-man rush. However, it is not always the same seven. Rushers can come from all angles (see Blitzes under pass rushes).

       The three, deep secondary men cover man-to-man on their receivers. One other player, to be named, will cover the back out man-to-man if he releases.

    2) The "5-Blitz" (Right End) Stunt. Right end covers first back out if he releases. (See Figure 49)

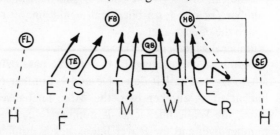

Figure 49 The "5-Blitz" (Right End) Stunt

3) Other types of "Blitzes" that can be used are 1 Blitz (Left End), 2-Blitz (Sam), 3-Blitz (Mike), 4-Blitz (Willie), or a 6-Blitz (Rover). (Refer to pressure team stunts.)

d. The "All" Stunts

On "All Blitz" everyone rushes except the three deep secondary. The ends must *crash* through the backs and eliminate them as potential receivers. (See Figure 50)

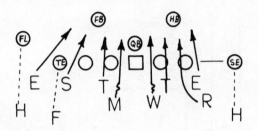

Figure 50 The "All Blitz" Stunt

C.P.: Ends, if backs set back, rush and crush. If they swing outside, adjust best way you know how. Keep outside leverage on the back. The "All" call can work with any of the basic stunts. Example, "All In." (See Figure 51)

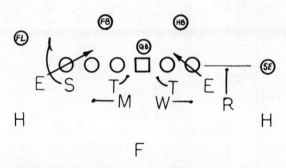

Figure 51 The "All In" Stunt

5. End Calls

a. The "Heads" Call. If flanker gives end a nasty split, he should give Sam a "Heads" call. This will move Sam further outside so that he can help the end contain without getting cut off by the tight end.

For easy reference, all End Stunts are listed by category in Table I.

END STUNTS (RIGHT AND LEFT)

Individual	Unit	Group	Team
End "Zip"	In	Rover and Sam In	Blast Right
End "Hold"	Out	Rover and Sam Out	Blast Left
	In Back	Rover and Sam Pinch	Dogs
	Pinch	* Also any of end's unit	Blitzs
	Stack	stunts in conjunction	All
		with one other unit stunt.	

* Combinations are too numerous to list; refer to the stunts.

Table I End Stunts

HOW TO COACH SPLIT-PRO
3 STRONGSIDE LINEBACKER
TECHNIQUES (SAM)

The "Sam" position is perhaps the toughest position for the coach to fill. Sam should be big enough and strong enough to handle the tight ends, down block, and neutralize the off-tackle power play. He should also possess the speed to cover backs out man-to-man on passes. This is a lot to ask of any player.

A player with these qualities is hard to find. Usually, the coach will have to settle for less qualified personnel at this position. However, with the numerous defensive variations and stunts listed in this book it is easy to adjust to the personnel available.

In the past, two types of players have been used successfully at the "Sam" position. They are the tackle type and the linebacker type. The tackle type can hold up well against the power off-tackle plays, but his pass coverage responsibilities must be kept to a minimum. The linebacker type of player is more capable of covering the backs out on passes, but on the other hand he must stunt more often in order to hold up against the off-tackle power plays.

It may be worth noting here that the key to good coaching is to be able to cover up the weaknesses and take advantage of the strengths of the personnel available.

A. General Concept:

Sam aligns over the tight end and will flip-flop from side to side if the tight end alternates his alignment from side to side. Sam assumes an upright two point linebacker stance over the tight end unless given a "down" call. On a "down" call Sam drops to a four point stance and digs in against the running game. Under certain circumstances Sam

49

will switch positions with the end on his side and use basically the same techniques.

B. Sam's Rules for Alignment:

1. Go to the tight end side of the formation and align on the tight end.
2. Go toward a wing and line up on the tight end.
3. Go away from a split end, if both ends are split play a "me," "you," or "you close" position. (See Rover calls and alignments.)
4. Go toward a close slot and play on the slot man.
5. Go according to the scouting report.

C. Sam's Possible Playing Positions: (Indicated by Letters)

Sam's alignments are indicated by letters for easy identification and communication purposes. Seven possible playing positions are listed below. The "I" and "H" positions are the basic alignments while the others are used for variation and special situations.

1. The "I" Position (Inside)—Basic: Sam lines up with the nose on the inside ear of the tight end in a two point stance.
2. The "H" Position (Heads)—Sam lines up head-on, eye to eye, nose to nose, on the tight end.
3. The "O" Position (Outside)—Sam lines up on the outside shoulder of the tight end.
4. The "D" Position (Down)—Sam lines up in a 3 or 4 point stance on the inside ear of the tight end.
5. The "L" Position (Loose)—Sam lines up in a 2 point stance 1½-2 yards off the ball.
6. The "S" Position (Stacked)—Sam stacks behind the defensive end (See Inside and Outside Stunt Calls)
7. The "W" Position (Walk Away)—Sam lines up in the flat, splitting the difference between the wide man and next man inside.

(See Figure 52 a, b, c, d, e, & f, for Sam's Alignments)

a) "I" Basic (Inside Ear)

b) "H" (Head-on)

c) "O" (Outside Shoulder)

d) "L" (Loose)

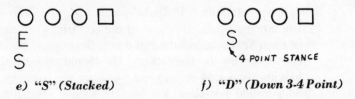

e) "S" (Stacked)   *f) "D" (Down 3-4 Point)*

Figure 52a, b, c, d, e, & f. Six of the Seven Possible Playing Positions for Sam (The seventh is self explanatory)

D. Sam's Basic Techniques and Variations:
 1. Sam's "I" Techniques:

   a. Purpose: The purpose of the "I" position is to plug the off-tackle hole and keep the tight end off of the inside linebackers.
   b. General Rule: Sam hangs tough in off-tackle hole.
   c. Alignment: Sam assumes an inside ear position on the tight end.
   d. Sam's "I' Stance:

    1) Basic: Sam lines up in a two (2) point stance with shoulders parallel to the line of scrimmage and twelve (12) inches off the ball. Sam should squat low, into a linebacker type stance, keeping the head up and arms low.
    2) In Short Yardage Situations: Use the "D" position (3 or 4 point stance)
    3) In Sure Passing Situations: Use the "H" position and hold up the end.
    4) In Prevent Situations: Use the "L" position (loose)

   e. Focal Point: Look through the tight end to the strong back and onside guard. (See Figure 53)

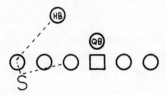

Figure 53 Sam's Focal Points

   f. Sam's Initial Movement ("I" Technique): Sam must always be mentally ready to defeat the down block by the end with a firm flipper. All moves should be made under control so that Sam will always end up in a good football position.

   On the snap of the ball, Sam takes a short jab step with the outside foot and delivers a hard flipper into the end, neutralizing his block.

g. Sam's Responsibilities ("I" Technique):

1) End attempts inside release—if the end tries to release inside of Sam, Sam squeezes the end down. Sam should never let the end inside on the linebackers. He should squeeze the play, looking for a lead or kick-out block by the backs or guards. Sam should not close too far. He should keep the outside foot planted, making it easy to react back to the outside.

2) End blocks down on Sam—if the end tries to block down, Sam should form tackle him, holding his position. If the ball gets depth and width, Sam should fight through the ends head and help outside. (See Figure 54)

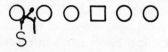

Figure 54 Sam's Reaction to End Blocking Down

3) End swings outside—if the end swings outside or influences Sam, Sam should take the initial step; looking to the inside. Sam should play off the end with the hands, looking for a lead block by the back, trap by the guard, or a turn out block by the tackle. Against a play inside, Sam reacts back inside, ready to play off the blocks by using an inside shoulder and forearm lift.

Basic Rule: Diagnose and hang in the off-tackle hole.

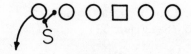

Figure 55 End Releases Outside of Sam

C.P.: Sprint out Sam's way, delay rush! (Depends on secondary coverage.)

4) End drops back—if the end drops back and pass protects— expect a delay route. Sam should grab him, and force him back, staying with the end if he tries to release, do not be a sucker for a slow block and cut-off. Sam must be alert for the screens, hides and sneak routes (delay type routes).

Figure 56 End Pass Protects

5) Responsibilities on Flow Away—Sam always executes the initial steps, stepping and chucking the end. If the end releases, react back and into a cushion, looking inside for the guard trap or tackle trap counter plays.
   a) No Counter—Cushion back through the hook area looking for a flaring halfback out the backside. Sam takes the throwback to the tight end or flare to the halfback. Sam also looks for the counter trap up the middle. (See Figures 57 and 58)
   b) No Counter or throwback—Sam takes the proper pursuit angle and helps on wide cutbacks.

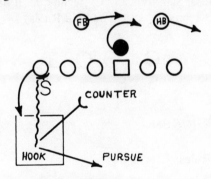

Figure 57 Flow Away from Sam—Cushion

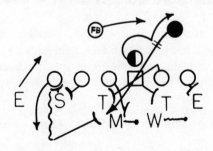

Figure 58 Sam's Reaction to a Counter Play

6) Review of Sam's responsibilities from the "I" position:
   a) Keep end off inside backer. Force the end to release outside.
   b) Close the off-tackle hole.
   c) Take quarterback on option. (Depends on what type of option play.)
   d) Vs. sprint out—delay rush! (Some cover calls require short, flat coverages by Sam.)
   e) Be alert for counters on initial flow away.
   f) Cushion for the throwback on flow away.
   g) Pursue on wide play away.
   h) Clothes-line any back releasing through the off-tackle hole or through the area.

2. The Sam Switch vs. a Nasty End Split: Vs. a nasty end split, Sam uses a "switch call" and applies regular split rules or stunts. (Depends on personnel; may not need the switch.) On a "switch call" Sam exchanges positions with the end and plays an "O" or "H" technique, depending on the distance of the split of the end. If the end plays close, Sam uses an "O" technique; if its a good split, Sam uses an "H" technique. (See Sam Split Rules)

S   E

Figure 59 Switch Call by Sam

3. Sam's Split Rules:

   a. If the offensive end splits 1-2 feet, Sam plays the end head up or in the "H" position.
   b. If the offensive end splits 2-3 feet, Sam plays on the inside eye or in the "I" position.
   c. If the offensive end splits 4-5 feet, Sam loosens slightly.
   d. If the offensive end splits 6 feet, Sam calls "switch" and switches positions with the end (the exact split to execute the switch will vary according to opponents). Sam now plays head up, up to 3 yards.

4. Sam's "Switch" Position Split Rules: (Sam switches positions with the end).

   a. If the offensive end splits 2-3 yards, Sam plays head up.
   b. If the offensive end splits 4 yards, Sam plays the inside shoulder.

c. If the offensive end splits 5 yards, Sam plays normal or plays head up and stunts to the inside.

5. The "Heads-Call" by the Defensive End. (Sam plays head-up on the end.) When the flanker gives the end a nasty split, the end may give Sam a Heads-Call, bringing Sam to a head-up position. See the "H" Technique.

a. Sam's "H" Technique: (Head-Up)

    1) Alignment: Nose on the tight end or slot back.

    2) Stance: Line up in a two point stance, shoulders parallel to the line of scrimmage 12-16 inches off the ball. Do not get too close. Squat low into a linebacker type position, ready to meet the end, with the head up and arms low.

    3) Focal Point: Through tight end to strong back and onside guard.

    4) Sam's reaction to movement:

        a) If the end comes at Sam—Sam form tackles him, setting himself, not taking one side or the other. He should stay head to head, stabbing the end up straight and forcing him back. When the play is clearly inside or outside, throw off the end and make the tackle.

        b) If the end blocks down or tries to hook Sam out, Sam closes inside, but not so far that he cannot help outside.

        c) If the end releases outside, Sam plays off the end with the hands, reacting back inside, looking for traps and leads. Flow away, Sam cushions and checks for counters and reverses.

    5) Purpose of the "H" Technique: Holds end up and gives added support outside. Can be an automatic adjustment in sure passing situations or called in the huddle.

6. The "L" Technique: (Loose)

a. Position: Sam plays a loose eagle-type position, 2-2½ yards off the line of scrimmage. (See Figure 60)

Figure 60 Sam's "Loose" Position

b. Purpose of the "L" Technique: For sure passing and prevent situations. Can be an automatic adjustment by Sam in prevent situations or called in the huddle.

7. Sam's "D" Technique: (A down, 3 or 4 point position)

   a. The "D" Technique vs. a Tight End: Sam lines up in a three (3) or four (4) point stance with the shoulders square to the line of scrimmage.
   b. Movement: At the snap, Sam lunges off, taking a short jab step with outside foot up and out into the end. Sam delivers as hard a flipper as possible on the end, looking inside for back leading or guard trap.
   c. The "D" Technique Position vs. a Slot: Line up head-on the slot. Sam should always be mentally ready to defeat the double team block by the end and slot back.
   d. Purpose of "D" Technique: Used for stopping a powerful off-tackle attack. Also used in the Split-6 Defense.

8. Sam's "O" Technique (Outside Alignment):
   a. Position: Align on the outside shoulder of the offensive end with outside foot back and use normal end assignments. Refer to end techniques for further explanations.
   b. Purpose of the "O" Technique: Used after a "switch" vs. a tight end. Also used in 50 defense.

E. Sam's Adjustments ("I" Position):
   1. Sam's Adjustment to a Close Slot—Sam lines up in the "H" position on the slot back. At the snap, Sam steps to the slot with the outside foot, mentally prepared to meet the slot's block or a double team from him and the end. Sam must not be caved in nor turned out.

F. Sam's "Basic" Pass Coverage Techniques:

   1. Basic Information
      a. Basic Rule: Delay the tight end and pick up the first back re-releasing to the outside.
      b. Stance: Regular
      c. Alignment: Regular
      d. Keys: Do not look at end; Sam can see the end and read the triangle at the same time (End, quarterback, and nearback) (See Figure 61)
      e. Sam's Special Calls: When a pass play is recognized Sam makes the proper call.

         1) When pass shows, call—"Pass, Pass, Pass."
         2) When the ball is thrown or fumbled, call—"Ball, Ball, Ball."
         3) When a pass shows and then develops into a run, call—"Run, Run, Run."
         4) When a screen develops, call—"Screen, Screen, Screen."
         5) If a draw develops, call—"Draw, Draw, Draw."

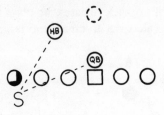

Figure 61 Sam's Keys

2. Responsibilities:
   a. Sam's Reaction to a Drop Back Pass:
      1) Do not let the tight end across and inside, pass or run. Play the tight end tough using bump-and-go techniques (See Secondary Attacking Techniques) on him until the near back releases. When the back releases, drop off and pick him up. Be alert for the screen pass.
      2) Sam can afford to get a little depth in the bump-and-go and still fall off in time to cover the back out.

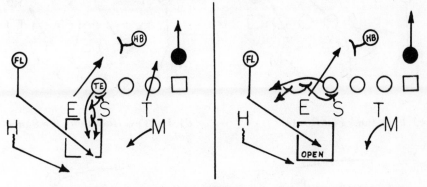

a) Correct Angle: Let the receiver release outside at about 45° into slant area.

b) Incorrect Angle: Over forcing opens the slant-pass and increases the end's chances of slipping back inside. (Be alert for inside spin release by the end.)

Figure 62a and b Sam's Bump-and-Go Techniques vs. the Tight End

      3) Sam picks up the wide flare (anything outside the end), keeping good leverage on the flaring back and encouraging him to move across the face. Sam always delays the tight end unless he receives a call from the safety releasing him of the delay technique. (See special calls—Plug.) Sam works the

"triangle;" if no back releases, he plays the end tough as long
as possible (alert not to create too large a void underneath).

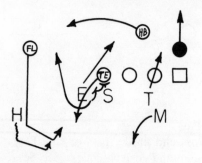

a) Vs. a Back Flare Route

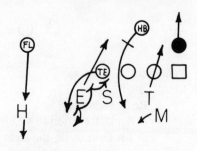

b) Vs. the Quick and Check Routes

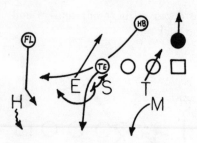

c) Vs. a Back Flat Route

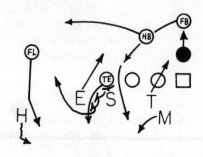

d) Vs. Two Backs out the Same Side

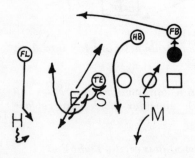

e) Vs. Two Backs Out the Same Side "Quick"

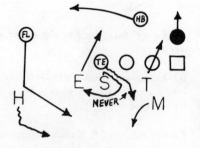

f) Sam Never Permits the End to Release Inside.

Figure 63a, b, c, d, e, and f Sam's Techniques for Picking up Backs Out of the Backfield.

STRONGSIDE LINEBACKER TECHNIQUES (SAM)   59

b. Sam's Reaction to a Sprint Out:
  1) Sprint toward Sam:
    a) Read defense—Sam rushes vs. the sprint out pass.

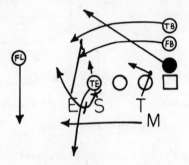

Figure 64 Sam's Reaction to Sprint Out (Read)

    b) Go defense—Sam stays with the end; then, picks up the
       first back out.

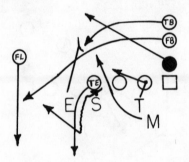

Figure 65 Sam Delays and then Picks up the Back Out on "Go Defense"

  2) Sprint away from Sam:
    a) Sam plays the tight end tough and remains with him all
       the way unless a back flares out the backside—must take
       throwbacks away. (Be alert for counters and reverses).
       (See Figure 66a and b)

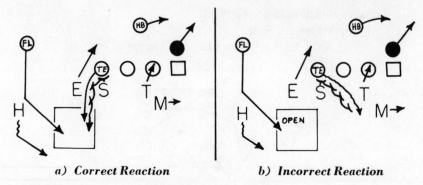

a) Correct Reaction   b) Incorrect Reaction

Figure 66a and b Sam's Reaction to Flow Away

G. Sam's Straight "Zone" Pass Coverage Techniques:
  1. Vs. a Dropback Pass:

  a. Do not let tight end across.
  b. Play the tight end tough for 2-3 yards; then release into the flat;
     take the flanker coming in, or the tight end going out. Must be
     alert for a screen.

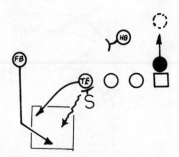

Figure 67 Sam's Zone Coverage Area

  c. Sam always gets depth as he backs out to shut off the quick slant-
     in area.
  d. Sam picks up flaring backs.
     Sam should keep good leverage on flaring backs, making them go
     across the face.

C.P.: Do not come up until ball is in the air.

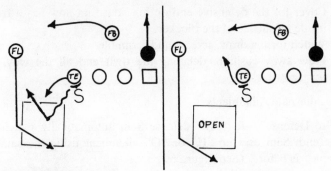

a) Correct Reaction by Sam
b) Incorrect Reaction by Sam (Picking up back too soon)

Figure 68a and b Sam's Reaction to a Dropback Pass-Zone Coverage

    2. Flow Away from Sam:
      a. Play the tight end real tough and do not let him cross in front. Drop straight back to hook area anticipating a throw back to the flanker on a slant inside. Also, look for the counter play. (See Figure 66a and b)

H. Covering Motion (Checking-Pro)
    (See covering motion in the secondary section)
    When the offensive team sends out a motion man, leaving only one running back in the backfield, the Mike linebacker will "Check-Pro." (See Check-Pro in Linebacker Section.) When the offense uses motion of this type they are trying to:

    1. Remove a backer so that they can hit up the middle with a quick trap, dive, or draw.
    2. Spread the defensive secondary thin, overload an area for passing, or force secondary rotation.

To counter this strategy Mike will make a "Check-Pro" call and the team will make the following adjustments:

    1. Tackles tighten down.
    2. Mike moves to the middle and plays a 4-3 linebacker.
    3. Willie drops out to Rover's position on the weakside.
    4. Rover adjusts as needed toward the flat or deep middle depending upon the direction of the motion.

Sam's Reaction to "Check-Pro" is as follows: (Delay rush)

    1. Remain in the same position.
    2. Chuck the tight end as before.
    3. Delay rush, keying remaining back on both sprint toward and dropback.

4. Cover for the defensive end on his side. End now has a free rush inside or outside of the blocker.
5. Watch for the draw, screen, and scramble.
6. Flow away cushion, delaying the tight end all the way. Watch for throwbacks.

I. Sam's Alternate Alignments:

1. "Pro Defense"—In "Pro" defense Sam automatically switches with the end. Sam uses an "H" or "O" alignment using the same techniques as before. (See Figure 69)

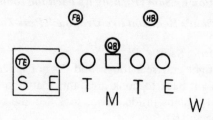

Figure 69 Sam's Alignment on "Pro" Defense (Sam Switch)

2. "Split-6" Defense—In the "Split-6" defense, Sam uses a three or four point stance in the "I" position plugging the off-tackle hole and rushing all passes.
3. "OH" Defense—Sam abandons regular rules and aligns head-on the center using read techniques. (See Nose Charge under Tackle Techniques)

J. Outside Linebacker Stunts
1. Sam's Individual Stunts (Sam Only)
   a. General Concept: Individual stunts refer to stunts that involve one player stunting while the rest of the defense plays regular.
   b. The "Sam Zip" Stunt
      1) Assignment: On "Sam Zip," Sam fires through the end and tackle gap, disregarding the tight end. Step with the outside foot first. Do not allow the tight end to cut you off. (See Figure 70)

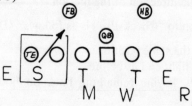

Figure 70 The Sam "Zip" Stunt

    2) Purpose of "Zip" Stunt: To insure good pass protection, some offensive teams will double on the tackles presuming that Sam will go back and out, covering the tight end. When this happens, the Sam "Zip" stunt will come free.

C.P.: The defensive end should pull the halfback outside, freeing Sam. The strongside tackle, if doubled, can now spin back to the inside because Sam will fill the off-tackle hole on the "Zip" stunt.

  2. Sam Unit Stunts (Sam and Onside End)
    a. General Concept: Sam can make the stunt calls (in some situations, an automatic stunt can be made by Sam at the line of scrimmage) or Mike can include the stunts in the defensive call. The calls tell the end what to do. Sam does the opposite.
    b. The "Sam In" Stunt: Sam's Rule—If "Sam-In" is called in the huddle, Sam should remind the end of the call as he aligns. (This goes for all stunts.)
      1) Stance: Regular
      2) Stunt: Draw block from the end and work outside, Sam cannot get hooked. Sam assumes the end's responsibilities; containing on all wide plays outside.
      3) Responsibilities:
        a) Flow Toward: Contain
          (1) Option: Take the pitch man, force quarterback to keep—fight for time and help.
          (2) Sprint Out: Force and Contain.
        b) Drop Back Pass: Read this while drawing the end's block, then:
          (1) If Zone: Cover flat.
          (2) If Man: Delay receiver; then, pick up first back to release outside.
        c) Flow Away: Cushion alert for reverses and counter plays.
      4) Basic Stunt Rule: Outside man has the Pitch and the inside man has quarterback. (See Figure 71)

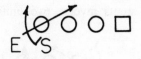

Figure 71 "Sam In" vs. a Tight End

    5) Purpose of "Sam In" Stunt: Breaks up the close wing and slot blocking combinations. Also destroys the option play.

c. The "Sam In Back" Stunt:

    1) Stance: Same as for "In."

    2) Stunt: Same as for "In," except that the end loops behind Sam.

    3) Purpose: Breaks up close wing and slot blocking combinations. Good vs. drop back pass protection.

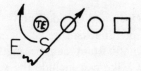

Figure 72 The "Sam In Back" Stunt vs. a Tight End

d. The "Sam Out" Stunt:

Used when Sam and the end are in the switched positions. Sam fills inside and off-tackle by looping behind the end. The end shoots across containing the outside plays.

Purpose of the "Sam Out" Stunt: Works well vs. a nasty split by the tight end. Also works well from the "You" alignment when both ends are split. (See Rover Calls and Alignments.)

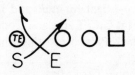

Figure 73 The "Sam Out" Stunt after a "switch" (Pro defense)

3. Sam Group Stunts

a. General Concept:

Group stunts will go by the same names. The only difference between Unit stunts and Group stunts is the number of units involved. Group stunts involve two units stunting at once. (See Figure 74)

Figure 74 The "Sam and Rover In" Stunt

4. Sam Team Stunts:
   a. General Concept:
   Team stunts are stunts that involve all units at the same time.
   b. The Blast Stunts:
   The blast stunt is an all-out rushing effort by one side of the line. The other side of the line plays regular defensive techniques. Sam's Blast Rule: Sam's side called, shoot guard and tackle gap. Other side called, play regular. (See Figure 75)

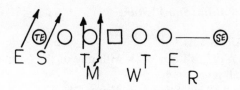

Figure 75 The "Blast Left" Stunt

   c. The "Dog" Stunts (Six-Man Rushes):
   On a "Dog" call Sam shoots the gap and rushes unless his name or number is called. If his name is called, he will cover the first back out on his side man-to-man. For further explanation of the names and numbers automatic system, refer to the dogs and blitzes section on defensive end play.
   Example: 26-Dog (Sam and Rover). (See Figure 76)

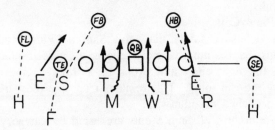

Figure 76 The "26-Dog (Sam and Rover)" Stunt

   Variations of the Dog Stunts: Could be a 24-Dog (Sam and Willie), a 23-Dog (Sam and Mike), or a 25-Dog (Sam and Right End).
   d. The "Blitz" Stunts (Seven-Man Rushes):
   Sam has the same rules on a blitz as on the dogs. Rush unless #2 is called, then cover the back out.
   Example: 2-Blitz (Sam) (See Figure 77)

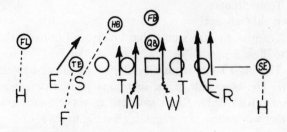

Figure 77 The "2-Blitz (Sam)" Stunt

e. The "All" Stunts
   The "All" call can work with any of the basic stunts. "All" refers to all units.
   1) The "All In" Stunt (See Figure 78)

Figure 78 The "All In" Stunt

K. Special Calls:
   1. The "Plug" Call:
      The defensive safety may give Sam a "Plug" call. When this happens, Sam is automatically relieved of pass responsibilities (delaying the tight end) and drops to a three or four point stance playing the run tough. This remains true regardless of Sam's alignment, switched or otherwise.
   For easy reference, all Sam Stunts are listed by category in Table II.

STRONG OUTSIDE LINEBACKER STUNTS (SAM)
Variations of a Basic Play: Regular and Switch

Individual	Unit	Group	Team
Sam Zip	Sam In	*Any Sam Unit Stunt used in conjunction with one other unit stunt.	Blast Right
	Sam In Back		Blast Left
	Sam Out		Dogs
	Sam Pinch		Blitzs
	Sam Stack		All

*Combinations are too numerous to list, refer to the Stunts.

Table II Strong Outside Linebacker Stunts—Sam

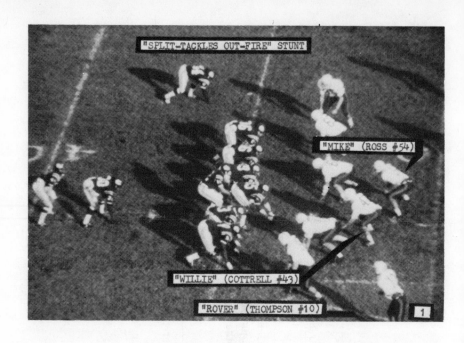

68

Split/Tackles Out-Fire

On this stunt, the tackles (Leonard Henderson #61 and Jack O'Donnell #77) loop out and into the offensive tackles using "read" techniques. The inside linebackers (David Cottrell #43 and Jack Ross #54) fire through the center and guard gaps. Note the good containing positions held by both the ends and the tackles.

4

HOW TO COACH SPLIT-PRO INSIDE LINEBACKER TECHNIQUES (MIKE AND WILLIE)

As in other defenses, the linebackers are the key individuals in the Split-Pro defensive system. The qualifications for Mike and Willie differ slightly due to assigned responsibilities.

The "Mike" backer should be the stronger of the two inside backers, as he is called upon to handle the power plays off-tackle and up-the-middle from both the split and Pro alignments. From the Pro alignment (a middlebacker position), Mike is expected to make the majority of tackles from sideline to sideline. The majority of the time Mike is free of pass responsibilities so that he can play the running game with all-out effort and enthusiasm.

Willie should be the quicker of the two inside linebackers as he is called on to play the weak, outside-linebacker position in the Pro defense. As a weak, outside linebacker, Willie is involved in pass coverage. Therefore, speed and agility, as well as tackling ability, are important here. Willie must also be strong enough to help Mike plug the middle of the line against wedge and power plays when aligned in the split defense.

A. General Concept.

In the split-Pro defensive system the "Mike" linebacker is the signal caller and will align on the strong side of the formation. The "Willie" backer will line up opposite the "Mike" backer. (See Post-Huddle Alignment in section on "Using the Split-Pro Defense".)

The inside linebackers have dual responsibilities supporting both the front line against runs and the secondary against passes.

71

B. Inside-Linebackers' (Mike and Willie) Techniques.
   1. Basic Alignments (Split Defense).
      a. The "Mike" Linebacker. Mike aligns on the strong side of the formation, over the offensive guard. Mike's position may vary with defense called and the offensive formation alignment. (See Figure 79 for the basic "Split" alignment.)
      b. The "Willie" Linebacker. Willie aligns on the weak side of the formation, over the offensive guard. Willie's position may also vary according to the defense called and the offensive formation. (See Figure 79 for the basic "Split" alignment.)

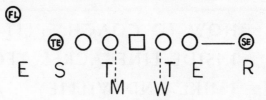

Figure 79 Inside Linebackers' (Mike and Willie) Alignment in "Split Defense"

   2. Basic Stance. The inside-linebackers' basic stance is a two-point, square stance with the knees bent, head up, and the back straight. Both Mike and Willie line up, heads-up, on the offensive guards. The distance off the ball is about 2-2½ yards off the line·of scrimmage (depending on the down and distance).
   3. Inside Linebacker Keys. The Inside linebacker keys may vary from game to game. The basic keys are the offensive guards, center, and quarterback.
      a. Stunting Keys. If a middle stunt is called, the linebackers should key the center and the ball. On stunts that aim linebackers outside of the defensive tackles, the linebackers should cheat toward the target just slightly before the ball is snapped.
      b. Other Keys That Can Be Used. The ball, the backs, the quarterback, the center, or the guards (depends on the scouting report).
   4. Inside-Linebackers' Basic Types of Play.
      a. Inside-Linebackers' "Split Go" Techniques.
         1) Purpose of the "Go" techniques. They provide a forcing and attacking type of linebacker and tackle play.
         2) The "Go" techniques.
            a) Backfield Flow Toward Backer. When flow is toward the inside linebacker, he will scrape (take a lateral step, then penetrate up field) and attack the offensive tackle on the side of flow. If no tackle is in the area, the line-

backer takes on the backs, guard or quarterback, whichever comes first. The linebackers should keep their
shoulders square to the line of scrimmage at all times.
(See Figures 80a and b and 81a and b)

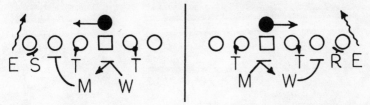

a) Flow Toward "Mike"   b) Flow Toward "Willie"

Figure 80a and b Inside Linebackers' Reaction to Flow Toward—"Go"

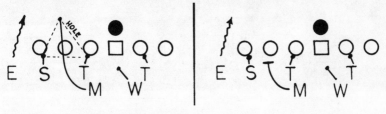

a) Flow Toward "Mike" Incorrect Reaction (Over Penetration)

b) Flow Toward "Mike" Correct Reaction

Figure 81a and b Inside Linebackers' Incorrect and Correct Scrape
Techniques When Flow Is Toward

b) Backfield Flow Away from Backer. When flow is away
from the backers, the backer will attack the center ex-
pecting a counter play. If the center tries to cut the backer
off, he should fight through his head and to the outside.
(See Figure 82)

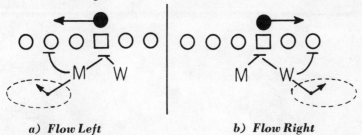

a) Flow Left   b) Flow Right

Figure 82a & b Inside Linebackers' Correct Fill Techniques on Flow
Away

c) On Flow up the Middle. When flow starts up the middle,

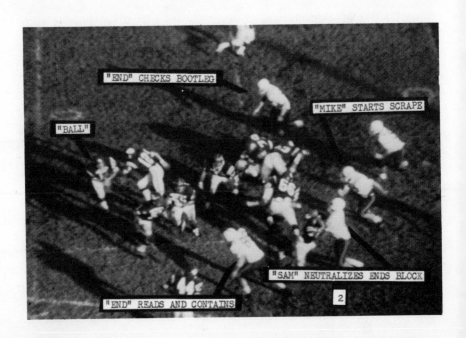

"END" TRAILS

"BALL"

"MIKE" FREE TO MAKE TACKLE

"END" (ELDRIDGE # 88) REMOVES INTERFERENCE

3

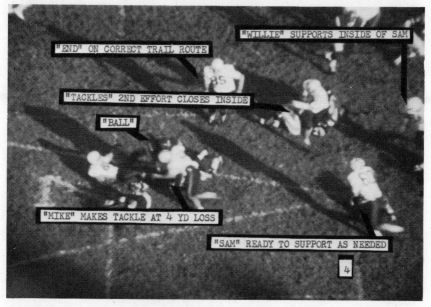

"WILLIE" SUPPORTS INSIDE OF SAM

"END" ON CORRECT TRAIL ROUTE

"TACKLES" 2ND EFFORT CLOSES INSIDE

"BALL"

"MIKE" MAKES TACKLE AT 4 YD LOSS

"SAM" READY TO SUPPORT AS NEEDED

4

"Split-Go" Defense vs. the Green Bay Sweep

Tackles (Jack O'Donnell #77 and Ed Irby #75) execute a "Go" charge which makes them vulnerable to the down blocks of the offensive center and strongside tackle. However, the "Mike" linebacker (Jack Ross #54) can now scrape free of resistance. The end (Don Eldridge #88) helps by removing the interference and pulling up the ball carrier while Sam (Chuck Weigl #60) neutralizes the tight end's block and positions to support the run outside or inside as needed. As a result "Mike" makes the tackle four yards deep in the backfield. (Central State vs. Northeastern.)

the inside linebackers stuff, squeeze, and jam the middle area. The linebackers should take on the center with the inside shoulder, keeping the outside arm free.

b. Inside Linebackers' "Split Read" Techniques
  1) Purpose of the "Read" Techniques. The "read" techniques work well for inside traps and in long-yardage situations (does not provide a good pass rush).
  2) Linebackers' "Read" Techniques.
    a) Flow Toward Backer. When flow is toward the backer, he should shuffle laterally down the line. If a large hole appears, take it; otherwise, shuffle on to the outside. He must be careful not to overrun the ball carrier (work the inside hip).
    b) Flow Away From Backer. When flow is away, shuffle laterally to a position head-up on the center, checking for the counter play. If no counter, shuffle on down the line, alert for cut back—watch angle of pursuit. If a pass shows, go back and to the outside at 45° into the hook area, looking for the tight end (or halfback). If no one threatens the hook area, move to the curl area and help as needed. (See Figure 83a and b)

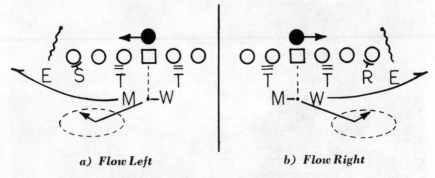

a) Flow Left   b) Flow Right

Figure 83a and b Inside-Linebackers' "Read" Techniques

  c) On Flow up the Middle. When flow starts up the middle, the inside linebackers stuff, squeeze, and jam the middle area.

c. Inside-Linebackers' "Split-Shoot" Techniques
  1) Purpose of the "Shoot" Techniques. The "shoot" techniques work well when the offense attempts to block down (away from flow) with the center to cover for a pulling guard. The shoot technique is also effective against slow developing outside plays.

2) The "Shoot" Techniques:
   a) Flow Toward Backer. When flow is toward the inside linebacker, he should shuffle down the line using the same techniques as in the "Read." (See Figure 84a and b)
   b) Flow Away From Backer. When flow is away, the linebacker should shoot the center-guard gap. Crash through the line the best way possible and chase the play from behind. (See Figure 84a and b)

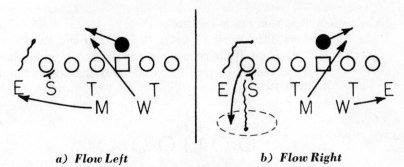

a) Flow Left   *b) Flow Right*

Figure 84a and b Inside-Linebackers' "Shoot" Techniques

   c) Flow up the Middle. When flow is up the middle, the backers react the same as for "Go" and "Read."
d. Variations of Basic Types of Play
   1) "Tackles Go—Backers Read" Techniques
      a) The tackles play "go" techniques.
      b) The inside backers (Mike and Willie) play "read" techniques. (See Figure 85.)

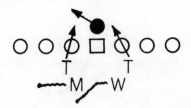

Figure 85 "Tackles Go—Backers Read" Techniques

   2) "Tackles Read—Backers Go" Techniques
      a) The tackles play "read" techniques.
      b) The inside linebackers (Mike and Willie) play "go" techniques. (See Figure 86)

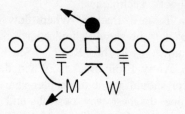

Figure 86 "Tackles Read—Backers Go" Techniques

5. Coaching Points on Inside-Linebackers' Play.
   a. Linebackers' Play Against Center Blocks (Go and Read)
     1) "Go" Defense. If the center fires out at the backer, he should meet the center, keeping the inside area free—fight through the center's head.

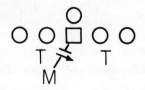

Figure 87   Linebackers' "Go" Techniques Against Center's Cut-off Block

     2) "Read" Defense. If the center fires out to cut the backer off, the backer should pound the center's helmet with the heel of the back-side hand. Drive the center's head down and into the ground, keeping him off the legs.

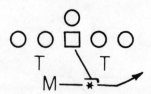

Figure 88   "Read" Techniques Against Center Cut-Off Block

   b. Linebackers' Reaction to a Sprint-Out ("Read" Techniques). When sprint-out key develops, the linebackers sprint to their zones; when quarterback sets up, they set up. If the quarterback decides to run the ball, the backers should sprint to within three yards of the quarterback, break down into a good football position and make the tackle (use the sideline).

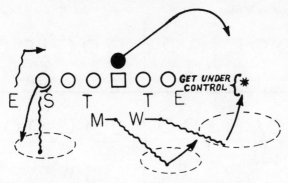

Figure 89 Linebackers' Reaction to Sprint-Out Pass and Quarterback Keep

   c. Inside-Linebackers' Reaction to Counter Plays (Go and Read Techniques)

     Both inside linebackers must be continually alert for the counter-trap plays. More time than usual should be spent practicing against the type of trap illustrated (Figure 90). The inside linebackers must learn how to read counter-plays. Sometimes it helps to mentally analyze the backfield set and determine which back will be the counter man if flow is away.

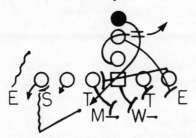

Figure 90 The Troublesome Counter Trap

C. Controlling Excessive Line Splits

     The inside linebackers are responsible for controlling the splits of the two guards. If the guards split out, increasing the distance between the tackles, the backers can make an adjustment or stunt on them until they reduce. If the backer wants the tackle to take the guard gap, he will call "gap." If he taps the tackle on the outside hip, he will move inside and take the guard-center gap. The linebackers adjust accordingly. (See Figure 91a, b, c, and d)

NOTE: The backers "fire and deal" stunts will also discourage large line splits.

D. Inside-Linebacker Pass Coverage—Split Defense.

   1. Inside-Linebackers' Reactions to a Drop-Back Pass.

a) "Gap" call by Willie   *b) Willie "Tap"*

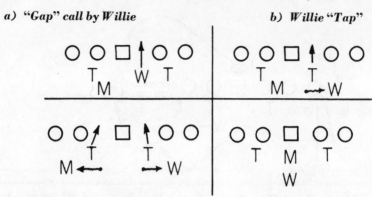

c) Willie and Mike "Taps"   *d) Check "Nose"*

Figure 91a, b, c, and d Adjustments to Excessive Line Splits

a. Special Calls. After recognizing a pass, the inside linebackers should make a call and react simultaneously.

1) When a pass shows, call "Pass, Pass, Pass."
2) When the ball is released, call "Ball, Ball, Ball."
3) If pass shows and then develops into a run, call "Run, Run, Run."
4) If a pass develops into a draw, call "Draw, Draw, Draw."
5) If a pass develops into a screen, call "Screen, Screen, Screen."

b. Responsibilities against Drop-Back Pass

The responsibilities of the inside linebackers against the drop-back pass are as follows in sequence:

1) Recognize the pass key as quickly as possible.
2) React out and back at a 45° angle.
3) Locate the near back, thinking "draw" on the first and second steps.

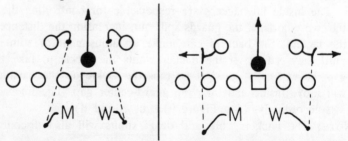

a) Draw—Backer should locate near back; if he sets or moves closer to quarterback, think "Draw."

b) Screen—If back moves away from quarterback, look for screen.

Figure 92a and b Reading the Draw and the Screen

4) Locate #2 receiver (the second eligible receiver from the outside) and read his route as well as the near back's. (Receivers are numbered one through three from the outside in on both sides).

5) If #2 or #3 receiver releases and fights to get inside, take him on in hook zone (knock receivers around).

6) If both #2 and #3 receivers release outside, get to the curl zone, looking for the #1 receiver coming toward the middle. If he attempts a cross route, deck him on the spot.

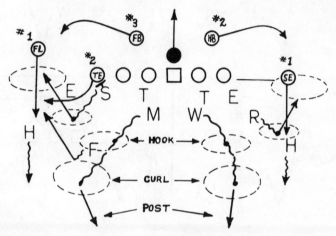

Figure 93 Inside-Linebackers' Reaction When Number 2 Receiver Releases Outside

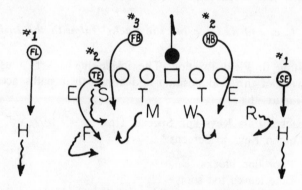

Figure 94 When Number 2 or Number 3 Receiver Releases Inside. (Pull up in the Hook Zone and Attack People.)

2. Covering Backs Out. (See Figure 95a, b, c, and d)

a) Halfback Quick up the Middle on the Tight End Side of the Formation

b) Halfback Quick up the Middle on the Split End Side of the Formation

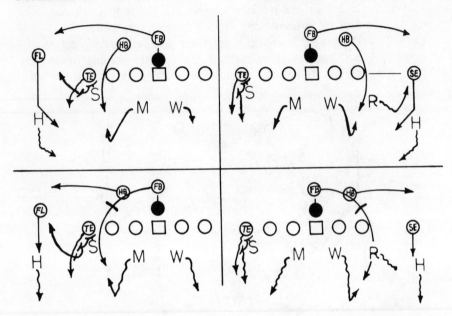

c) Fullback Check Through on the Tight End Side of the Formation

d) Fullback Check Through on the Split End Side of the Formation

Figure 95a, b, c, and d. Covering the Backs Out with the Inside Linebackers

3. Adjusting to Field Position. The inside linebackers must always be aware of the field position and adjust their paths accordingly. (See Figure 96)

4. Linebacker Pass Keys and Special Tips
   a. Common Keys to Screens

   1) Poor line blocks
   2) Line leaves too soon
   3) Back releases (poor block on end)
   4) Quarterback gets too much depth (over 7 yards)
   5) Two backs release to the same side
   6) Fake draw

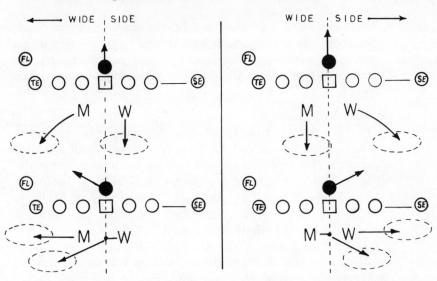

a) Ball on the Right Hash Mark   *b) Ball on the Left Hash Mark*

c) Ball on the Right Hash Mark   *d) Ball on the Left Hash Mark*

Figure 96a, b, c, and d. Inside Linebackers' Adjustments to Field Position on Passes

    7) If all backs release, locate the tight end!

  b. Linebackers' Special Pass Tips

    1) As you break huddle, look and locate your hook zone; find the spot and know where to go if pass develops.

    2) If it is a drop-back pass, get to the proper zone—eye quarterback and near halfback, on first and second steps looking for the draw.

    3) If draw comes, close it in, keeping outside in leverage and yelling, "Draw, Draw."

    4) Look for screen if the quarterback delays the throw.

    5) If pass develops, go to the hook zone; if no one is there or threatening, go to the curl zone.

  5. Special Calls Involving the Linebackers

    a. The "Gone" Call. A "Gone" call by the Rover tells the onside backer that he must pick up the onside back (regardless of action) if he releases for a pass.

    b. The "One" Call. A "One" call by the Rover tells the onside backer that if play action is away and the onside back releases on his side, he will have to cover him for the throwback. On all other actions, the Rover will pick him up. (Just one action gives Willie coverage on back.)

  c. The "Two" Call. A "Two" call by the Rover tells the onside backer that he has the onside back in case of pass if play action is away or a drop-back. On flow his way he has no pass responsibilities. (Two actions give Willie pass coverage on the onside back.)

 6. Covering Motion

The "Check-Pro" Call (from Split Defense). On motion by outside people (wing, slot or flanker), the secondary will make the adjustments (Rover, Halfbacks and Safety). On motion by remaining backs, Willie will move out (to the weak side of the formation) and call "Check-Pro." It is the responsibility of Willie to make this check call—the responsibility of tackle positioning is placed upon the Mike linebacker (stunts, etc.)

When motion begins, Willie will yell, "Check-Pro" and replace the Rover who now moves to the flat or deep 1/3 area, depending on direction of motion. (See Secondary Play)

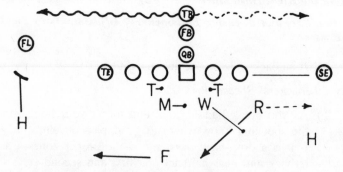

Figure 97 "Check-Pro" Adjustment to Motion

E. Inside-Linebackers' Alignments in "Pro" Defense

 1. General Concept. "Pro" defense resembles a standard 4-3 alignment. This defense is used in two ways—as a basic defense and as an automatic.

At times, "Pro" defense can be used as an automatic ("Check-Pro" call) to compensate for a man in motion.

Calling the defense:

a. Huddle Call: "Pro" Defense

b. If used as an automatic: "Check-Pro"

 2. Willie-backer's Alignments and Assignments in "Pro" Defense.

a. General Concept. Pro-defense moves Willie to an outside linebacker position on the weak side of the offensive formation.

b. Willie's Stance. A two-point stance in a good football position, with the inside foot forward, the outside foot back and shoulders square to the line of scrimmage.

Willie's alignment will vary. His basic alignment is 2½ to 3 yards outside the offensive tackle and 2½ to 3 yards off the line of scrimmage. At times Willie will be asked to play a walk-away or a heads position. Refer to Rover positions in the Rover section of this book for further explanations.

c. Willie's Most Common Alignments.

1) The Basic Alignment. Willie's basic alignment in "Pro" defense is a position 2½ to 3 yards deep and 2½ to 3 yards outside of the tackle on the split-end side.

Willie's assignments (when offensive end is split out) are to give the end a "You" or a "Me" call (this gives the end his assignment) and play accordingly. The choice of calls depends upon the tactical situation and scouting report.

a) The "You" Call. Willie supports inside of the end against a run if a play threatens that area. The end contains.

b) The "Me" Call. Willie supports outside of end and contains all end runs if a play threatens that area. The end plays tough inside.

Figure 98 Willie's "Basic" Pro Alignment

2) The "You Close" Alignment. Give the end a "You" call and line up over the tackle one and a half to two yards off the line of scrimmage. Use a tough linebacker technique on the tackle (extra low and dig in).

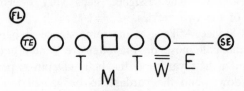

Figure 99 The "You Close" Alignment

3) The "You Walk" Alignment. Give the end a "You" call and align half way between the split end and defensive end. Stay

far enough off the line of scrimmage that the look-in pass and the flat zone can be covered easily.

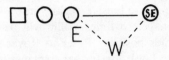

Figure 100 Willie's "You Walk" Position

    4) "Pro-Willie Stack." On a "Willie Stack" call, Willie stacks behind the end and works the "in and out stunts" or the standard "you or me" calls. The choice of calls depends upon the tactical situation and the scouting report.

Figure 101 Willie's "Pro-Willie Stack" Position

    5) The "Force" Position

        When "Force" is called (automatic in some defenses), Willie moves up on the line of scrimmage, just outside of the end and gives the end a "Me" call. Willie now contains and the end plays tough to the inside.

3. Mike-backer's Alignments and Assignments in Pro Defense

    a. General Concept. Pro-defense moves Mike to the middle line-backer position. When in this position, Mike has a "two-gap responsibility." The assigned gaps vary depending upon the stunts of the two tackles.

    b. Mike's Stance. Mike uses the same stance as before, but centers upon the ball, nose on the offensive center and about two to two and a half yards off the ball. (Depth depending upon the stunt, down, and the yardage to be gained.) The closer Mike aligns, the lower the stance should be.

    c. Focal Point. Focus through the center and two guards to the offensive backs. Read their movements and react accordingly, keeping in mind the assigned gaps.

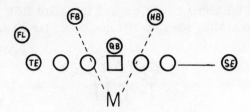

Figure 102 Mike's Focal Points in Pro-Defense

d. Movement:

1) If one or both guards pull and the center attempts to cut Mike off, he should play through the center's head and work down the line of scrimmage with the flow. While shuffling down the line, Mike should keep the shoulders square and stay behind the ball, alert for the cut back.

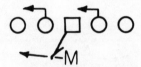

Figure 103 Mike's Reaction to a Center's Cut-Off Block

2) If the center drives straight at Mike, Mike should meet him nose on, not taking a side until the ball is located, then pursue.

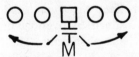

Figure 104 Mike's Reaction to a Play up the Middle

3) If the center blocks out on the tackle and the guard pulls, Mike must be ready to meet the guard or tackles down block. In meeting the block, Mike should play through the guard's head, then pursue with the flow.

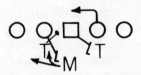

Figure 105 Mike's Reaction to the Guard's Block

4) If the center blocks out and the guard folds up through the hole, Mike steps up and neutralizes the guard's block.

Figure 106 Mike's Reaction to the Fold Block

5) On pass key, Mike gets to the proper zone alert for draws and screens. (Zone will depend on the coverage call.)

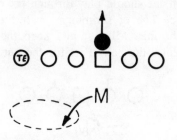

Figure 107 Mike's Reaction to a Drop-Back Pass

F. Inside-Linebackers' Stunts and Stunting Techniques
   1. General Concept:
      The split-defensive alignment presents so many good stunts that there is a tendency for the coach to include too many in the defensive game plan. Keep the stunts limited, do not take away the team's aggressive instincts by overloading their minds with numerous stunts, checks, and alignments. The final selection of stunts to be used depends on the blocking combinations used by the opponent; therefore, they may vary from week to week. Exercise great care in selecting stunts—they can win for you if they are used correctly.
      The defensive signal caller (Mike) must take great pride in his responsibilities and study like an offensive quarterback. If a competent signal caller cannot be found, work out a signal system and let the coach call them. This allows Mike to play an aggressive type of football without mental congestion (thinking too much). (See Defensive Organization and Strategy.)
   2. Inside-Linebackers' Individual Stunts (One Backer Only)
      a. The Mike "Fire" Stunt. Mike shoots the center and guard gap while Willie draws the center's block. The tackles use a "read" technique, being outside conscious first.

Figure 108 The Mike "Fire" Stunt

C.P.: Position on the field determines which backer will fire. Usually the backer on the short side of the field fires.

    b. The Willie "Fire" Stunt. Willie shoots the center and guard gap while Mike draws the center's block. The tackles use a "read" technique, being outside conscious first.

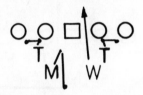

Figure 109 The Willie "Fire" Stunt

C.P.: On stunts the linebackers should:

1. On inside stunts, key the ball. At the snap, shift the eyes to backfield for the action.
2. On a pass, rush all out with the hands high.
3. On a run, stop one yard deep in the backfield and go into pursuit from there.
4. If the ball is midway between hash marks, stunt according to formation and opponent's tendencies. If ball is on the hash mark stunt according to field position. Linebacker on the short side of the field fires (varies with the scouting report).

3. Inside-Linebackers' Unit Stunts (Both Backers involved)

    a. "Backers Fire" Stunt. Both linebackers shoot the center and guard gaps while the tackles use a "read" technique, being outside conscious first.

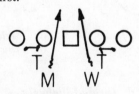

Figure 110 The "Backers Fire" Stunt

C.P.: When both inside linebackers are stunting, the tackles should look hard for the draws and screens (tackles use "read" type techniques).

    b. "Backers Fire-X" Stunt. Mike always fires first, Willie fires second. This stunt, like the others, can be used in the pro-defense with no change in assignments.

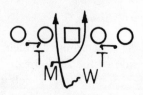

Figure 111 The "Backers Fire-X" Stunt

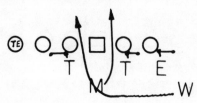

Figure 112 The "Pro-Backers Fire-X" Stunt

    c. "Backers Fire on Flow" and the "Willie Gap-Fire" Stunts.

a) "Backers Fire on Flow"   *b) "Backers Fire on Flow"*

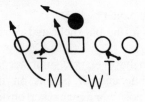

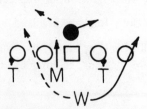
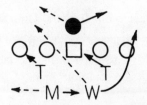

c) 70 Mike Gap (for 70 defense,   *d) Tackles Slant—"Willie Fire*
see short yardage defenses)—   *on Flow"*
"Mike Fire on Flow"

Figure 113a, b, c, and d. Inside-Linebackers' "Fire on Flow" Stunts (Split and 70 Mike Gap Defenses)

d. The "Mike Deal" Stunt. A "deal" is a stunt between one backer and the tackle on his side. The tackle takes the center and guard gap while the backer fires the guard and tackle gap.

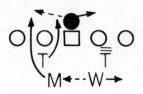

Figure 114 The "Mike Deal" Stunt

e. The "Willie Deal" Stunt. The tackle on Willie's side works the inside gap while the Willie backer fires through the guard and tackle gap.

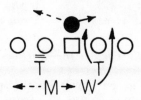

Figure 115 The "Willie Deal" Stunt

Coaching points: Linebackers' shooting and dog techniques

The stunting linebacker can use the inside hand to feel for center and the outside hand to feel for guard. Knife through with inside leg first, keeping the shoulders square. This way, once the inside leg is through the gap, the guard can only bump the back leg. This should not completely cut the linebacker off from outside pursuit.

4. Inside Linebackers' Group Stunts (Two Units Stunting—Usually Backers and Tackles)

a. "Tackles In—Backers Read or Fire" Stunts. The linebacker can play two ways in coordination with the tackles stunts—backers can use read or fire techniques; can also be one or both backers. Purpose: Plugs inside ice (isolation), trap, and power plays between the guards. Also gets linebackers started outside.

a) "Tackles In—Backers Read"
(Backers step outside and read
the play)

b) "Tackles In——Backers Fire".
(Backers shoot the guard and
tackle gaps)

 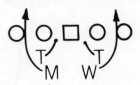

c) "Tackles In—Willie Fire"
(Mike reads and Willie fires
through the guard and tackle
gap)

d) "Tackles In—Mike Fire"
(Willie reads and Mike fires
through the guard and tackle
gap)

Figure 116a, b, c, and d "Tackles In—Backers Read or Fire" Stunts

b. "Tackles In—Fire on Flow" Stunt. If play action is toward the linebacker, he will "Fire." If play action is away from the backer, he will use "Read" techniques. On fire stunts the backers always go through the gaps uncovered by the tackles.

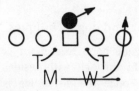 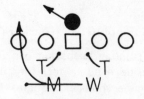

a) Flow Right   *b) Flow Left*

Figure 117a and b "Tackles In—Backers Fire on Flow" Stunt

c. "Tackles In—Mike or Willie Fire" Stunts. If the inside linebacker's position name is included in the stunt called, he "fires." If backer's name is not included in the call, he will use "read" techniques.

C.P.: Stunts should be used according to formation and field position.

a) *"Tackles In—Mike Fire"*   b) *"Tackles In—Willie Fire"*

Figure 118a and b "Tackles In—Mike or Willie Fire" Stunts

    d. "Tackles Out—Backers Read or Fire" Stunts. The inside backers now cover the inside gaps using techniques called for, read or fire.

a) *"Tackles Out-Read" (Backers hesitate and be ready to fill middle)*   b) *"Tackles Out-Fire" (Backers shoot the guard and center gaps)*

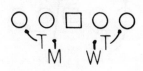
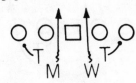

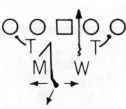
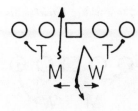

c) *"Tackles Out—Willie Fire" (Mike fakes fire and then reads, Willie fires guard and center gap)*   d) *"Tackles Out—Mike Fire" (Willie fakes fire and then reads, Mike fires guard and center gap)*

Figure 119a, b, c, and d "Tackles Out—Backers Read or Fire" Stunts

    e. "Tackles Out—Shoot" Stunt. (See "Shoot" techniques in Linebackers' Basic Techniques section)

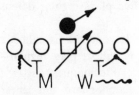

a) *Flow Right*   b) *Flow Left*

Figure 120a and b "Tackles Out—Shoot" Stunt

f. "Tackles Slant (Liz or Rip)—Backers Read or Fire" Stunt. Mike gives a "Liz or Rip" call at the line of scrimmage which gives the tackles their direction to slant; the call depends on the offensive formation and scouting report.

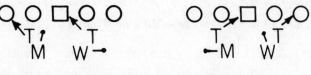

a) "Liz"   *b) "Rip"*

Figure 121a and b "Tackles Slant—Read" Stunt

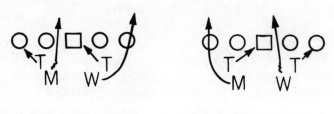

a) "Liz"   *b) "Rip"*

Figure 122a and b "Tackles Slant—Fire" Stunt

a) "Tackles Slant—Willie Fire"   *b) "Tackles Slant—Mike Fire"*
Stunt   *Stunt*

Figure 123a and b "Tackles Slant—Mike or Willie Fire" Stunt

5. Inside-Linebacker Team Stunts (Stunts Involving the Team)
   Team stunts are stunts that involve all units at the same time.
   a. "Blast" Stunts. The blast stunt is an all-out effort by one side of the line. The other side of the line plays regular defensive techniques.
   The Linebackers' "Blast" Rule: If your side is called, shoot the center-guard gap. If other side is called, play regular—be alert wide toward the blast stunt (use read techniques).
      1) "Blast Right" Stunt. (Willie shoots guard and center gap and Mike plays read.)

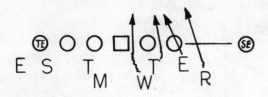

Figure 124 "Blast Right" Stunt

2) "Blast Left" Stunt. (Willie reads and Mike shoots the guard-center gap.)

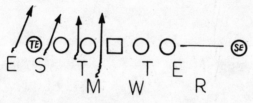

Figure 125 "Blast Left" Stunt

b. Inside Linebackers' "Dog" and "Blitz" Principles

On a "dog" or a "blitz" call, the linebackers shoot the gaps (Fire) unless their names or numbers are included in the call (outside rushers contain). If their numbers 3 and 4 (Mike-3 and/or Willie-4) are included in the call (such as "34-Dog), they will cover the first back out their side man-to-man. If both backers are dogging, they can use straight fire, fire-X, slant fire, or in and out fire techniques. (See Figures 110, 111, 116b and 122)

If the opponents use more than one offensive formation or backfield set, as most teams do, the defensive signal caller (Mike) may have to use an automatic call at the line of scrimmage (the backfield may shift from one set to another, so an automatic system for calling the dogs and blitzes is a must if maximum results are expected). The above remains true for the blitz stunts also. (See "attacking the protection" in the defensive strategy section.)

1) At-the-Line Automatics for the Dog and Blitz Stunts.

In order to effectively automatic to any of the dogs at the line of scrimmage, each possible pass defender is given a number. If Mike calls a defender's number, he will cover the first back releasing on his side. If his number is not called, he is free to rush using the dog rush techniques. When using this system, all the signal caller (Mike) has to do is make a huddle call of "dog" or "blitz" and then make a two-digit

"SPLIT/ALL-IN" TEAM STUNT VS. A SPRINT OUT PASS

"SAM" (WEIGL #60)   "END" (ELDRIDGE #88)

1

"SAM" LOOPS OUTSIDE & CONTAINS

"END" CRASHES INSIDE

2

"SAM " CHECKS SPRINT DRAW

"END" CHECKS SPRINT DRAW

"END" (DIXON #85) CHECKS FOR COUNTER & REV.

3

96

The "Split/All-In" Team Stunt vs. a Sprint-Out Pass

The ends (Don Eldridge #88 and Richard Dixon #85) and tackles (Jack O'Donnell #77 and Ed Irby #75) crash hard to the inside while Sam, the strongside linebacker (Chuck Weigl #60), loops outside to contain. The inside linebackers Mike (Jack Ross #54) and Willie (David Cottrell #43) move outside to cover for the guard and tackle gaps, then react to the play. Due to good secondary coverage on this particular play Sam and the trail end knock the quarterback out of bounds for a five-yard loss.

97

number (or one for a blitz) call at the line of scrimmage to match the offensive set.

2) Number Assignments for Dogs and Blitzes. Numbers are assigned to the eligible pass defenders, from left to right. The left defensive end is number one, the Sam linebacker is number two, the Mike linebacker is number three, the Willie linebacker is number four, the right end is number five, and the Rover linebacker is number six.

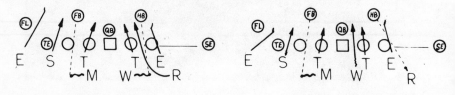

a) 34-Dog (Backers)   b) 36-Dog (Mike and Rover)

Figure 126a and b "Dogs" Involving Backers in Pass Coverage

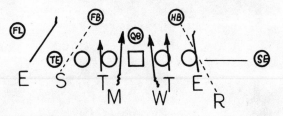

Figure 127 26-Dog (Sam and Rover) Stunt

Coaching Points: Backers' Pass Coverage Techniques on the "Dogs."

If a backers' name or number is called, he should cheat late to a headup position on the back he is assigned to. He should mirror the back wherever he goes, looking for draw, flare and screen—"eyeball" the back. If the back releases through the line, the backer should tackle, knock, or cut him to the ground—eliminating him as a receiver. (See Figures 128 and 129)

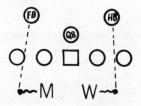

Figure 128 34-Dog (Backers) Stunt

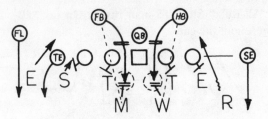

Figure 129 Linebackers' Tackling Against Turnout Protection Blocking (Eliminates the release valve and the hot routes.)

c. Inside-Linebackers' "Blitz" Stunts (7-man rushes). The inside linebackers have the same assignments on a blitz as they do on a dog. If the backer's name or number is called, he will cover the back out (first back out either side on a blitz stunt.) If his name or number is not called, he will shoot the gap and get the quarterback.

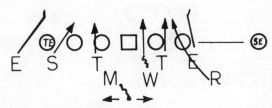

Figure 130 3-Blitz (Mike) Stunt

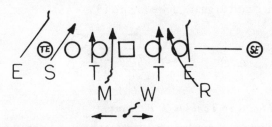

Figure 131 4-Blitz (Willie) Stunt

d. The "All" Calls
   1) "All-In" Stunt. On "all-in" stunt, the inside linebackers step outside and cover the uncovered gaps. If a pass develops, they will cover the backs out.

Figure 132 The "All-In" Stunt

2) "All-Blitz" Stunt (8-man rush). On the "all-blitz" the backers shoot the gaps.

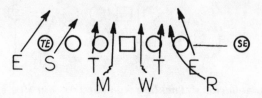

Figure 133 The "All-Blitz" Stunt

6. Mike's Stunts from the Pro Alignment

All basic split defensive stunts can be used in the pro-defense.

a. "Pro-Tackles In" Stunt. The tackles are responsible for the guard and center gaps while Mike fills the guard and tackle gap on the side toward flow. (See Figure 134)

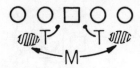

Figure 134 The "Pro-Tackles In" Stunt

b. "Tackles Out" Stunt (Use Sparingly). The tackles are responsible for the guard and tackle gaps while Mike fills the middle area from guard to guard. (See Figure 135)

Figure 135 The "Pro-Tackles Out" Stunt

c. "Pro-Tackles Slant" (Liz and Rip). On the tackles slant stunt the tackles slant into the gap toward Mike's call, "Liz" for left and "Rip" for right. Mike covers the two gaps left open by the call.

 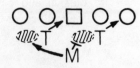

a) Slant—Liz   *b) Slant—Rip*

Figure 136a and b The "Pro-Tackles Slant" Stunt (Liz and Rip)

d. "Pro-Tackles Pinch" Stunt. On a pinch stunt the tackles pinch the guards looking for the middle quick trap or the wedge play up the middle. Mike covers, favoring the two outside gaps.

e. "Pro-Tackles In—Fire on Flow" Stunt. The tackles will execute the "In" stunt and Mike will fire the guard and tackle gap toward the side of backfield flow.

a) Flow Left   *b) Flow Right*

Figure 137a and b The "Pro-Tackles In—Fire on Flow" Stunt

f. "Pro-Backers Fire" Stunt. Same as in Split defense, just go from a different alignment.

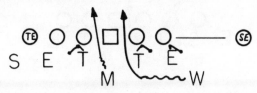

Figure 138 The "Pro-Backers Fire" Stunt

g. "Pro-Backers Fire-X" Stunt. Same as in Split defense, only go from the Pro alignment.

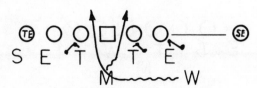

Figure 139 The "Pro-Backers Fire-X" Stunt

h. "Pro-Tackles Slant—Backers Fire" Stunt.

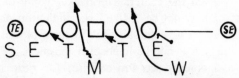

Figure 140 The "Pro-Tackles Slant—Backers Fire" Stunt

7. Inside-Linebackers' Alternate Alignments and Stunts.
   a. The "Fifty (50) Defense." Inside linebackers widen slightly (until they are positioned over the guards).

Figure 141 The "Fifty (50) Defense"

b. The "Seventy (70) Defense." Willie or the Mike backer moves to the center-guard gap. Can be a "70-Mike Gap" or "70-Willie Gap."
   1) "70-Mike Gap." Mike moves late to strongside center and guard gap. Willie aligns in normal split position.

Figure 142 The "70-Mike Gap" Defense

   2) "70-Willie Gap." Willie moves late to strongside center and guard gap. Mike aligns in normal split position.

Figure 143 The "70-Willie Gap" Defense

c. The "Nose" Defense. Willie or Mike moves to a four (4)-point stance, nose on the center. The backer going to the down position may or may not be "Mike," depending on physical qualifications; it may be wise to substitute a third tackle. The remaining backer plays the middle-linebacker position. (For middle-linebacker assignments see Pro-defense; for nose assignments see Tackle Play and the Nose Charge Technique.)

Figure 144 The "Nose" Defense

Stunts from "Nose" Defense:
1) "Nose—Mike Fire" Stunt. Mike shoots same gap called for in the split defense—backers fire stunt. Mike uses a jump and twist technique, sliding sideward through the gap giving the center and guard a small target. Willie uses read techniques.

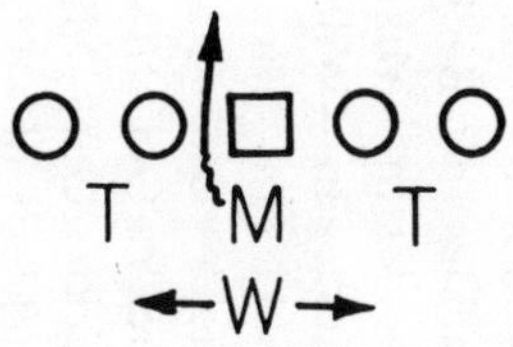

Figure 145 The "Nose—Mike Fire" Stunt

2) "Nose—Backers Fire" Stunt. Mike shoots same gap as before; Willie shoots the other gap.

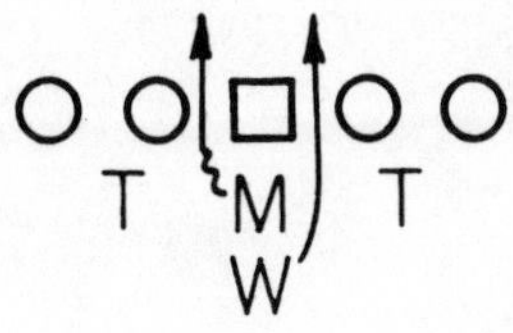

Figure 146 The "Nose—Backers Fire" Stunt

For easy reference, all inside linebacker stunts are listed by category in Table III.

INSIDE LINEBACKER STUNTS (MIKE AND WILLIE)

Variations of Basic Play: Read, Go, and Shoot.

Individual	Unit	Group	Team
Mike Fire	Backers Fire	Mike Deal	Blast Right
Willie Fire	Backers Fire-X	Willie Deal	Blast Left
	Backers Fire on Flow	Tackles In—Backers Read	Dogs
		Tackles In—Backers Fire	Blitzs
		Tackles In—Mike Fire	All
		Tackles In—Willie Fire	
		Tackles In—Fire on Flow	
		Tackles Out—Backers Read	
		Tackles Out—Backers Fire	
		Tackles Out—Mike Fire	
		Tackles Out—Willie Fire	
		Tackles Out—Fire on Flow	
		Tackles Slant—Backers Read	
		Tackles Slant—Backers Fire	
		Tackles Slant—Mike Fire	
		Tackles Slant—Willie Fire	
		Tackles Pinch—Backers Read	

Table III Inside Linebacker Stunts—Mike and Willie

5

HOW TO COACH SPLIT-PRO
TACKLE TECHNIQUES
(RIGHT AND LEFT)

The defensive tackles, due to their alignment, will face a number of double-team blocks. Therefore, they should possess good size and strength, so that they can handle and break double teams. They will also face a number of combination blocks such as folds, crosses, traps, leads, and wedges; so, reaction and reading ability are also desirable qualities.

Like any other position, explosive power and quickness are extremely important for stunting and pursuit purposes.

A. General Concept

The defensive tackles' assignments are to cause blocking problems for the offensive guards and tackles. The defensive tackles should be able to defeat the single block efforts by the offensive guards and tackles, forcing them to double team. If the tackles can cause enough problems, the offense will be forced to use some type of a double-team blocking scheme. This, in turn, will free the inside linebackers so that they can move freely through their lateral pursuit lanes.

Other assignments for the defensive tackles include rushing the passer (again strive to force a double-team blocking scheme) and supporting against the running game inside and outside from sideline to sideline.

The defensive tackles have two basic types of play, "read" and "go." The "read" call provides a loose reading type of play, where the tackles hit, neutralize, control, locate the ball, and then pursue. The "go" call provides a more aggressive type of play, where the tackles crowd the ball, attacking the man in front and defeating him on his side of the line.

In the stunting defenses, the tackles are asked to shift laterally from one alignment to another, loop right or left, or slant right or left.

107

B. Defensive Tackle Play.
    1. Split "read" tackle techniques.
        a. Alignment: The tackles line up nose on the outside shoulder of
        the offensive guards (depends on split of the offensive guards)
        and about 12–18 inches off the ball. Contrary to the current
        trend, the tackles line up with the shoulders square to the line of
        scrimmage (some coaches angle their tackles to the inside).

        When the tackles set at an angle, they are easily down blocked
        by the tackles, and easily reach blocked by the guards. Also, the
        angle alignment decreases the defensive tackles' ability to "read"
        and react to various offensive tackle and guard combination
        blocks (crosses, folds, etc.).

        If the tackles remain solely in the basic starting position (de-
        cribed above), it might increase the possibility of a successful
        trap play up the middle. However, with various stunts (Pinch,
        In, Out and Slant) the chances are not as great as they may seem.
        b. Stance: The tackles assume a four-point stance with no more
        than a toe to instep stagger. The hips should be slightly higher
        than the shoulders.
        c. Focal Point: The tackles' initial keys are the offensive guards and
        tackles. They should use split vision and read the offensive
        guards' and tackles' blocking patterns so that they can make the
        correct reaction.
        d. Movement: On the snap of the ball, the tackles step to neutralize
        the blocks and read the blocking patterns for a key to the direc-
        tion of the play.

        The tackles should step, deliver a good blow, and then read.
        They must protect the guard and tackle gaps, not letting the
        guards get a hook block or a turn-out block. In protecting the
        guard and tackle gaps, the tackles must keep the shoulders square
        to the line of scrimmage.

        If the backfield flow is laterally down the line either way, the
        tackles work down the line of scrimmage taking a good angle of
        pursuit.

C.P.: The tackles should not spin out of double-team blocks; this will
only clog the linebackers' lateral pursuit lanes. (See Figure 148)

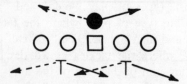 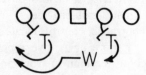

Figure 147 Tackle Pursuit Angles

Figure 148 Incorrect Reaction by Tackles. (The spin out clogs the line-backers' pursuit lanes)

If the onside tackle spins out, he may clog the linebackers' lateral pursuit lane. If the backside tackle spins out, his back will temporarily be to the ball; and as a result, he may not see a counter-play back to his side. However, the spin technique may be used sparingly against the drop-back pass or with the "shoot" type of play. (See Shoot Techniques)

e. "Read" Techniques: Use hard hands and forearms; otherwise, play soft and read.

1) If the guard or tackle attacks, the defensive tackle must neutralize, control, and work against the pressure, keeping the feet and shoulders parallel to the line of scrimmage. Against a cut off block, fight through the blocker's head by striking the blow and then going.

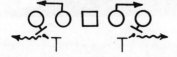   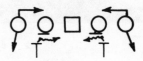

a) The Tackles Attacking the Tackles   *b) The Guards Attacking the Tackles*

Figure 149a and b The Defensive Tackle Reacting to Guard and Tackle Blocks

2) Fighting the Double-Team Block. The defender being double teamed should execute a near shoulder dip and nose dive aimed at the inside knee of the drive blocker. He should then immediately follow through by using the offside leg as the driver, coming up and through the double team, building a pile with the two blockers.

   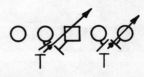

a) Fighting Pressure Left   *b) Fighting Pressure Right*

Figure 150a and b Fighting Double-Team Blocks

3) When the Guard Releases Inside. When the guard releases inside, look for the trap by the opposite guard or tackle. (Many offensive coaches like the tackle trap against the split alignment.) Squeeze the area down, meeting the trapper with the outside shoulder. Keep the inside arm free to make the tackle.

A SPECIAL "SPLIT-GO" TENDENCY DEFENSE (TACKLE CHARGE TECHNIQUES)

1

"ROVER" IN SPECIAL POSITION TO COUNTER THE QUICK PITCH

#61 HENDERSON (T) EXECUTES A "READ" CHARGE

"BALL"

#77 O'DONNELL (T) EXECUTES A "GO" CHARGE

2

"Split-Go" Tackle Charge Techniques

This series of photos shows the "Split-Go" defense with special adjustments to the split-end side to counteract offensive tendencies from this particular backfield set (this game only). The Rover backer (Phil Thompson #10) was moved to a special position to take away the crack block, the quick outside pitch and

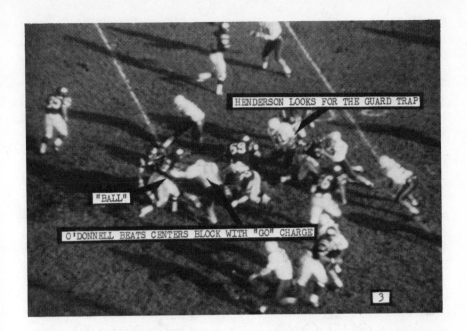

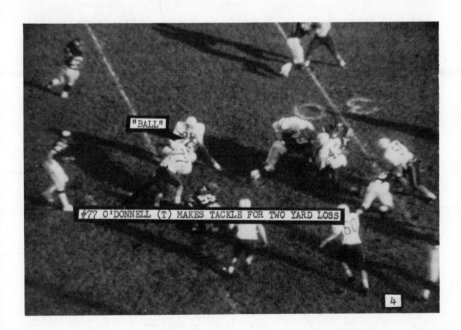

quick sideline pass. The right tackle (Leonard Henderson #61) uses a "Read" charge to counter the guard trap while the left tackle (Jack O'Donnell #77) uses a "Go" charge to beat the center's backside block. As a result, O'Donnell makes the tackle for a two-yard loss.

2. Split "Go" Tackle Technique
   a. Alignment: Same as for "read" only move up on the line of scrimmage. Get all of the ball possible, raising the hips slightly.
   b. Assignment: Attack the offensive guard; explode into him recklessly.
   c. Movement: When the ball moves, explode into the guard's outside shoulder. If he pulls, try to bump him off his route.

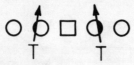

Figure 151   Tackle "Go" Techniques

d. Techniques:
   1) If the guard pulls, the tackle should get into his hip pocket and go with him.

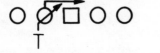   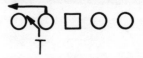

a) Get Into His Hip Pocket   *b) Run Around His Block*

Figure 152a and b   Tackle's Reaction to a Pulling Guard

   2) If the guard attacks the tackle, the tackle should meet and defeat him.
   3) If the guard pass blocks, the tackle should knock him back and into the quarterback.
   4) Against trap plays, the tackles must stuff the hole with the trap blocker.
3. Tackle "Shoot" Techniques.
   Alignment and Assignments: The tackle's alignments and assignments are the same as for "read" except that the tackles are allowed to use the roll-out technique if flow is toward them. (Against single or double-team blocks). The reason this is possible is because the backside linebacker will not need to pursue behind the tackles. (See Figure 153)

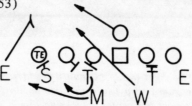

Figure 153   Tackle "Shoot" Techniques

C.P.: Before spinning, the tackle must neutralize the blocker's block. Then spin and pivot on the foot nearest pressure, throwing the opposite leg and elbow around the blocker.

4. Split "Pinch and Trap" Techniques.
   a. The "Pinch" Techniques.
      1) Alignment: The tackle lines up six inches off the ball and at a slight angle to the inside (tail out and head in).
      2) Assignment: Drive through the near neck area of the offensive guard. This decreases the area between the two tackles clogging the middle.
      3) Purpose: Helps against traps and power plays up the middle, but hinders outside pursuit by giving the offensive tackle the down block and the guard a reach block. Also hinders the reading of guard and tackle blocking patterns.
   b. The "Trap" Technique. On a "trap" call, the tackles align at a 45-degree angle and use the same charge as in the pinch call above.

5. Tackles "Check Pro" Alignment.
   When the Mike backer checks "pro" the tackles tighten down. In so doing, they should be alert for a trap, draw, or quick hitting play up the middle. (Depends on the backfield alignment.)

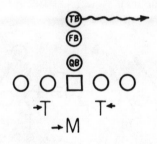

Figure 154 The "Check Pro" Adjustment

When the offensive team puts out two wideouts and sends one of the remaining backs in motion, they limit themselves to one running back. When they do this, they are trying to remove a linebacker so that they can either hit up the middle with a fullback trap or quick dive, spread the defensive secondary thin, or overload an area for passes.

In either case, in "check pro" the defense remains sound outside and inside. The tackle charges in the "pro" alignment are the same as those in the split defense (Read, Go, Pinch, etc.).

6. Special Tackle Charge

The "Nose Charge" ("50" alignment): The defender aligns head-up (6–12 inches off the ball), and delivers a good shoulder lift, then holds. He does not take a side until the ball carrier commits. The defender has a "two-gap" responsibility, the center and guard gaps.

Figure 155 The "Nose" Charge

C. The "Dog and Blitz" Pass Charges.

On a Dog or Blitz call the tackles can move late or cheat to a head-up position on the guards so that they can go either way off their blocks. They must:

1. Charge on the snap.
2. Put on the all-out rush.
3. Get to the quarterback the quickest way possible.
4. React to the run the best possible way.
5. Use the best pass rushing technique for the situation. (See Tackle Pass Rush Techniques)

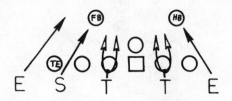

Figure 156 The Tackle "Dog and Blitz" Charges

C.P.: The Gap alignment is not always the best position from which to rush the passer since the offense can easily double team with tackle and guard. Cheating late to a head-up position on the guards may help the cause.

D. Special Calls Involving the Tackles.

At times the linebackers will make special calls directing the tackles to a new alignment. The tackles should be aware of possible calls and react accordingly, remembering that they work independently with the backer on their side.

If a linebacker wants the tackle on his side to move to the guard and tackle gap, he will call "gap" and tap him on the inside hip. If a linebacker wants the tackle to move to the center and guard gap, he will call "center" and tap the tackle on the outside hip.

The tackles will always move away from the hip that is tapped by the linebacker.

E. Rushing the Passer.
　1. General Concept.
　　　Again, the split defense is designed to "make things happen" and "force the big play." When this happens, the offense will be confronted with long yardage situations and be forced to throw the football. Therefore, the tackle pass rush is extremely important and must be effective.
　2. Rushing the Passer.
　　　When a pass shows—(normal pass rush): The tackles must get into the middle of their pass rush lanes and to the blockers before they can balance up and get set.
　　a. Right tackle. Start the charge through the outside shoulder of the guard. Get to the middle of the guard and work through him, gaining ground. Don't move laterally. Be alert for draws and screens.
　　b. Left tackle. Get head up on the guard and work through the middle of him. Force a double team by being too tough for the guard to handle. Be alert for the draw and screen.

C.P.: If a "Sam Zip" stunt is called and a pass shows, the tackle can automatically spin inside if doubled. Draw the blocks first.

　3. Pass Rushing Techniques.
　　a. The "Outside Shoulder Drive." Blast into the outside shoulder of the blocker (keep shoulder under his) and defeat his block. This is an all-out effort to physically overpower the offensive man.
　　b. The "Fake and Club." Fake one way or the other, club the helmet toward the fake. Rush the passer with hands high.
　　c. The "Butt and Go." Butt the blocker in the chin, as he braces himself, grab his jersey and arms just below and behind the shoulder pads. Throw him off and rush the passer with the hands high.
　　d. The "Hand Blow and Club." Drive at the blocker, delivering a hand blow into chin, helmet or chest; almost at the same time, come across with the other hand into the helmet with a club technique.
　　e. The "Spin." Used when the blockers attempt to double team. Drive hard into the blockers and then spin out, rushing the passer with the hands high.

Split-Read Tackles Alignment

Tackles (Jack O'Donnell #77 and Leonard Henderson #61) in the "Split-Read" alignment. Notice their position off the line of scrimmage. From this position they can easily read the blocking patterns of the offensive guards and tackles. (Central State vs. Northeastern)

Figure 157 The Tackle "Spin" Technique

4. Keys to Rushing the Passer:
   a. Strive to gain ground on the passer, decreasing his area of operation.
   b. Attempt to force the quarterback into another rusher or out of the pocket and into the ends.
   c. If the passer sets up looking through your lane, don't leave your lane, continue the rush.
   d. If the passer sets up looking through another lane, be reckless with your rush.

116

e. Key the depth of the quarterback's drop. If the quarterback gets deeper than seven yards, look for the screen.

f. When the quarterback gets his hands up to throw, get your hands up.

g. The tackles' goals are, in this order: (1) cut the vision of the quarterback in 2.9 seconds, (2) get his attention, (3) knock down the ball, (4) tip the ball or force elevation of the pass.

h. If you jump, come back down in the same tracks you left. This will give you the balance to react laterally if the scramble is on.

i. If you get to the passer, come down over the top of him pinning his arms to his side.

j. Special note. If passer gets more than seven yards deep, put on the brakes and look for the screen—start a good angle of pursuit.

F. Tackle Stunts—Split Defense

    1. Special Note.

On "fire stunts" where the tackles are not called into the stunts, tackles are to execute a read technique, playing soft and to the outside.

Example: "Backers Fire" Stunt.

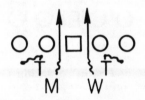

Figure 158 Tackle Play on "Backers Fire" Stunt

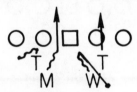 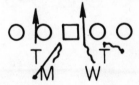

a) "Mike Fire" Stunt   *b) "Willie Fire" Stunt*

Figure 159a and b Tackle Play on "Mike and Willie Fire" Stunts

    2. Individual Stunts.

The "You and Me" Principle: Used mainly with the Pro-Defense in sure passing situations. The left tackle makes the call if no stunt is called.

a. The "You and Me" Tackle—plays for the draw and screen.

b. The Other Tackle—uses an all-out rush technique if a pass shows.

3. Unit and Group Stunts (In, Out, Slant, and Deal).
   a. The "In and Out" Stunts:
      1) Alignment. Cheat late to a head-up position on the guard.
      2) Assignment.
         a) Loop to the area assigned (guard and tackle gap or guard and center gap).
         b) The angle of the loop is determined by the alignment.
         c) The first step is the most important. Never let the man you are moving away from cut you off.
         d) Read on the move, reacting to pressure.
         e) If a lineman you are moving toward pulls, get into his hip pocket and follow. If he pulls opposite, pivot flat on the second step and pursue.
         f) If a pass shows, straighten up and get into a reckless pass rush.
   b. The "Slant" Stunt: If a "Slant" stunt is called for, the Mike backer will give a line call of "Rip" (right) or "Liz" (left). This gives the tackles the direction of their slant.

Figure 160 The "In, Out, and Slant" Stunting Techniques (Figure shows left tackle's In charge and right tackle's Out charge.)

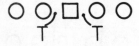

a) The "In" Stunt

b) The "Out" Stunt

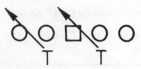

c) The "Slant" Stunt (Liz)

d) The "Slant" Stunt (Rip)

Figure 161a, b, c, and d The "In," "Out," and "Slant" Stunts

   c. The "Slant" Stunt Coaching Points: The direction of the slant is determined by a "Liz" or "Rip" call at the line of scrimmage by the Mike linebacker. This call tells both tackles which way to slant. The tackles key the man they are stunting toward.

Tackle "Slant" Techniques—the tackle steps with the onside foot feeling for guard with hands. If the guard blocks on the tackle, the tackle should spin back at the guard, countering with the hands. Quickness is a must.

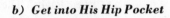
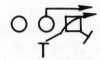

a) Butt Him in the Face Like a Goat

b) Get into His Hip Pocket

c) Recon or Spin Out—Flow Away

d) Rush the Passer

Figure 162a, b, c, and d Reacting to Blocks from the "Slant" Stunt

    d. The "Deal" Stunts (Mike or Willie): If a deal stunt is called for in the huddle, the tackles should be ready for the tap on the hip. After a tap, move into the gap away from the hip tapped. If no tap, use read techniques.

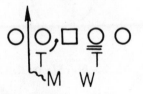

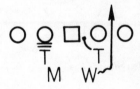

a) "Mike Deal"

b) "Willie Deal"

Figure 163a and b The "Mike" and "Willie" Deal Stunts

    4. Team Stunts.

      a. The "All" Calls: An "All" call means everyone is involved in the stunt called. The "All In" stunt is shown in Figure 164.

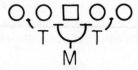

Figure 164 The "All" In Stunts

    b. The "Dog and Blitz" Stunts: On a "dog" or a "blitz" call, the tackles execute an all-out rush on the quarterback.

    c. The "Blast" Stunts

        1) Tackles' Rules for the "Blast" Stunt:

            a) "Blast Right" The right tackle shoots the gap between the guard and tackle. The other tackle plays a "read technique."

            b) "Blast Left" The left tackle shoots the gap between the guard and tackle. The other tackle plays a "read technique."

G. Tackle Stunts—Pro Defense.

    The stunts from Pro-defense are identical to those in the Split-defense. (See Figure 165, a, b, c, d, e, and f)

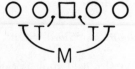

a) Tackles In

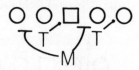

b) Tackles Out

c) Tackles Slant (Liz)

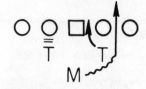

d) Tackles Slant (Rip)

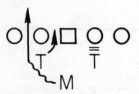

e) Mike Deal (Left)

f) Mike Deal (Right)

Figure 165a, b, c, d, e, and f The "Pro" Tackle Stunts

For easy reference, all tackle Stunts are listed by category in Table IV.

TACKLE STUNTS (RIGHT AND LEFT TACKLES)
Variations of Basic Play: Read, Go, and Shoot

Tackle-Individual Stunts	Tackle-Unit Stunts	Tackle-Group Stunts	Tackle-Team Stunts
You Me	In Out Slant	Mike Deal Willie Deal *Also any tackle unit stunt used in conjunction with one other unit that is also stunting.	Blast Right Blast Left Dogs Blitzes All

* Combinations are too numerous to list, refer to the Stunts

Table IV Tackle Stunts—Right and Left Tackles

H. Other Alignments.
   1. "Pro" Defense: If "Pro" defense is called, the tackles move to a head-up position on the guards. All stunts and charges are the same as for split defense. (In, Out, and Slant)
   2. "70" Defense (Mike and Willie Gap)
      a. 70-Mike Gap: The strongside tackle moves to a head-up position on the tackle and plays read techniques. (Can also slant through the tackle.) Weakside tackle remains in the same position. (See Figure 166)

Figure 166 "70 Mike Gap" Defense

b. 70-Willie Gap: The weakside tackle steps into and plays the offensive tackle. The strongside tackle remains in the split alignment and uses basic techniques. (See Figure 167)

Figure 167   The "70 Willie Gap" Defense

3. "Tight" Defense: The tackles move to a position slightly shading the inside of the offensive guards. The tackles key the guards and the ball. If the guard pulls to the inside, the tackles move laterally, playing through the center's head. (See Figure 168)

Figure 168   The "Tight" Defense

4. "50" Defense: On "50" Defense, both tackles move to an outside shoulder alignment on the offensive tackles. (See Figure 169)

Figure 169   The "50" Defense

6   HOW TO COACH WEAK OUTSIDE LINEBACKER TECHNIQUES (ROVER)

The Rover backer must be a good tackler who is capable of supporting the defensive end inside or outside, depending upon the call. Rover must also be agile enough to play pass defense man-to-man.

Rover can be classified as a combination linebacker and secondary defender.

A. General Concept.

The Rover backer will declare to either the right or the left of an offensive formation. The declared direction depends upon the secondary, color cover call. The two basic color calls are blue and red.

On a blue call, Rover aligns on the side away from the Sam linebacker. This is usually on the split-end side of the formation. If red is the cover call, the Rover will align on the same side as Sam. (See Secondary Coverages)

Once Rover declares, his exact position will depend on: the defense called, the coverage call, the formation, and the tactical situation.

At all times the Rover backer will give the end on his side a special call that tells the end what his responsibilities are. Rover's assignments are usually just the opposite.

B. The Basic Calls.

1. The "You" Call. On a "You" call the end contains the outside plays and the Rover fills inside of him. Rover does this by taking the initial steps, analyzing, and then reacting to the play.

2. The "Me" Call. On a "Me" call the end can move in tighter and play the off-tackle plays because the Rover now takes over his outside contain responsibilities.

3. The "Gone" or No Call At All. When assignments move the Rover away from the end's immediate support area, he should give the end a "gone" call. If the end receives no call or a "gone" call, he knows that he must contain because the Rover is removed from the area and cannot give quick help inside or outside against the run.

C. The Stunting Calls.

1. The "In" Call. On an "In" call, the Rover stunts outside, containing the wide plays. The end now crashes down hard through the shoulder and neck area of the last man on the line of scrimmage.

2. The "Out" Call. On an "Out" call, the Rover stunts hard through the shoulder and neck area of the last man on the line of scrimmage. The end now stunts outside containing the wide plays.

D. Rover's Alignments. As a general rule, Rover's exact alignment will vary according to the line formation, the backfield set, the tactical situation, and the scouting report. The basic rules for aligning are listed below.

1. Against a Tight End. Against a tight end Rover plays the same as the Sam backer. All keys and responsibilities are the same. Rover's basic alignment against a tight end is the "I" position. (See Sam's "I" Position) However, an automatic switch can be used if the Rover backer is not physically able to handle the "I" techniques. In short yardage situations, Rover can drop to the "D" position and plug the off-tackle hole. In sure passing situations, Rover can move to a head-up position on the tight end. For specific details as to techniques, refer to the chapter on Sam Linebacker Play and the "I" Position.

2. Against a Split End. Usually Rover will be confronted with a split end. In this case, Rover plays *one* of five different spots depending on the tactical situation, field position and the offense's tendencies.

a. The Force Position:

1) Concept: Rover supports outside of the end and contains the outside plays. The end can now play the off-tackle area hard. From this position Rover gives the end a "Me" call and plays accordingly.

2) Stance: Rover assumes a two-point stance with the inside foot forward and the shoulders square to the line of scrimmage.

3) Alignment: Rover moves to a position 1½ yards outside of the defensive end and up on the line of scrimmage.

4) Focal Points: Rover looks inside through the tackle to the quarterback and the near back. His reaction depends upon their direction of movement. (See Defensive End Techniques)

5) Initial Move: On the snap of the ball, Rover takes a short

T E R

W

Figure 170 Rover's Force Position

step forward with the inside foot, keeping the shoulders square to the line of scrimmage.

6) Responsibilities: (Read the Play Action)
   a) Run—Flow Toward:
      [1] If the ball remains on the line, make the quarterback keep the ball; but be in a position to get pitch man.
      [2] If the ball moves off the line, force and contain, squeezing the play to the inside.
      [3] If the ball moves up the middle, cushion back and to the inside.
   b) Run—Flow Away: Cushion back for throw back to onside end and the flare outside by the halfback.
   c) Pass—Flow Toward: Force and contain.
   d) Pass—Flow Away: Cushion back.
   e) Pass—Drop Back: Cover the flat.

b. The 2 x 2 Position.
   1) Concept: From the 2 x 2 Position Rover usually supports inside of the end while the end supports and contains the outside plays. From this position, Rover can also give the end a "You," "Me," "In," or "Out" call, depending on the situation.
   2) Stance: Same as "Me." (Give end proper call)
   3) Alignment: Two yards deep and two yards outside of the defensive end.
   4) Initial Move: On the snap of the ball, take a short jab step back with the outside foot. Rover reads the ball and the near back for next reaction.

T   E

W   R

Figure 171 Rover's 2 x 2 Position

5) Responsibilities.
   a) Run—Flow Toward:

        [1] If the ball remains on the line, hold the position and fill inside of the defensive end.

        [2] If the ball moves off the line, hold ground, ready to support inside first and outside second.

    b) Run—Flow Away:

        [1] If the ball moves up the middle, fall off inside and squeeze the play. Look for the counter play between the tackle and the guard.

        [2] If the ball moves outside, cushion back and pursue as needed. Be alert for reverses.

c. The "You Close" Position.

    1) Stance: Square. (Give end "You" call)

    2) Alignment: Over the weakside tackle and off the line in a loose position.

Figure 172 Rover's "You Close" Position

d. The "W" (Walk) Position. The "Walk" position is used for sure passing situations. From this position Rover will give the end a "Gone" call.

    1) Stance: Square or staggered with the inside foot forward.

    2) Alignment: Mid-way between the split receiver and the tackle.

    3) Focal Point: At the snap, be able to shift your view to the outside man expecting the crack block or the look-in pass.

    4) Assignments: Pass first, run second, and secondary contain responsibilities as needed.

C.P.: Be alert for a "crack" call from the defensive halfback. When this happens, he will force and contain while you work yourself back and outside to cover for him in case of a pass.

Figure 173 The Rover "Walk" Position

e. The "H" (Heads) Position (against a split receiver): The "Heads" position is used in sure passing situations to delay a good receiver.

1) Stance: Two (2)-point stance, weight evenly distributed on both feet, turned inside at a 45-degree angle. Can also be on the inside shoulder of the receiver, depending on the call from the defensive halfback. (See Secondary Section)

2) Alignment: Up on the line of scrimmage and on the outside shoulder of the outside receiver.

3) Focal Point: Look through the receiver to the quarterback.

4) Initial Move: On the snap of the ball, step into receiver and ride him off the line of scrimmage and to the inside for two or three steps. Analyze the play action at the same time.

5) Responsibilities:

    a) If a run develops toward you and the ball is on the line, take the pitch man.

    b) If the ball is off the line, react to the ball and support from the outside in.

    c) If the ball moves up the middle, support inside.

    d) When flow is away, cushion outside and take the proper pursuit angle to the ball.

E. Rover Stunts (Pro and Split Defense).

  1. General Concept: Stunts for the Rover are also broken down into various categories. They are: Individual, Unit, Group and Team stunts. On stunts that involve the end, the Rover will repeat the huddle call at the line of scrimmage reminding the end of his assignments.

  2. Rover Individual Stunts.

    a. The "Rover Zip" Stunt. On a "Rover Zip" stunt, Rover crashes the line of scrimmage expecting a sweep. In executing the stunt he should cheat to his assignment just before the snap of the ball. (See Figure 174)

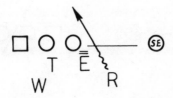

Figure 174 The "Rover Zip" Stunt

    b. The "Rover Heads and Zip" Stunt. Rover lines up in a "Heads" position on the split end. On the first verbal sound by the quarterback, Rover cheats inside and executes the "Zip" stunt at the snap of the ball. The key for executing the stunt may change from game to game.

  3. Rover Unit Stunts (Rover and End)

a. The "Rover In" Stunt. On an "In" stunt the Rover stunts outside and contains, while the end crashes through hip of the first man inside on the line of scrimmage. (See Figure 175)

□ ◯ ◯ ─ ⬤ SE
    T E
W   R

Figure 175 The "Rover In" Stunt.

b. The "Rover Out" Stunt. Rover shoots the guard and tackle gap while the end contains. Rover shoots the gap between the guard and tackle, taking on all action his way.
1. If the quarterback comes, take him on. If it is the belly option, take on the fullback and knock him into the quarterback, forcing a fumble or forcing him deeper outside. If the play gets outside, bow it up field and pursue. Against a sprint-out your way, get to the quarterback the best way you know how.
2. If the ball goes away, trail hard.
3. Against a dropback, you have a free rush on the quarterback.

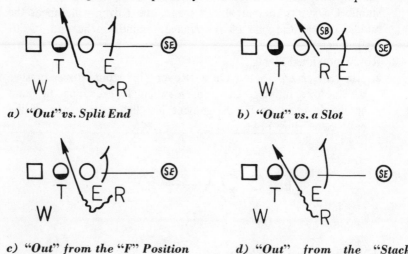

a) "Out" vs. Split End

b) "Out" vs. a Slot

c) "Out" from the "F" Position

d) "Out" from the "Stack" Position

Figure 176a, b, c, and d The "Rover Out" Stunt from Various Positions

4. Rover Team Stunts.
   a. The Dog and Blitz Stunts. Dog and Blitz refers to an all-out rush. If Rover's name or assigned number (6) is called, he will cover the back out on his side man-to-man. If Rover's name or number

(6) is not called with a dog or a blitz, he will shoot the onside guard and tackle gap.

1) When "Rover Dog" or "Rover Blitz (6)" is called, Rover will cover first back out on his side.

2) On any other Dog or Blitz call, Rover will shoot the guard and tackle gap. (For examples see the Dog and Blitz stunts listed in previous chapters.)

b. The "All" Stunts. An "All" call includes the Rover. For example: On an "All In" stunt, Rover executes the "In" stunt. On an "All Pinch" stunt, Rover executes the "Pinch" stunt.

c. The "Blast" Stunts (Blast Right or Left). If a blast stunt is called for on Rover's side, he can cheat up to a position on the line of scrimmage and crash to the outside hip of the nearest back.

F. Other Defenses:

1. The "Pro" Defense. When "Pro" defense is called for in the huddle, Rover will align in the free safety spot on the split-end side of the formation and play as the coverage call dictates. (See Secondary Coverages)

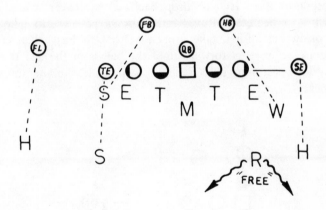

Figure 177 "Pro" Defense with Rover at the Free Safety Spot.

For easy reference, all Rover Stunts are listed by category in Table V.

WEAK OUTSIDE LINEBACKER STUNTS (ROVER)

Variations of Basic Play: You, You Close, Me, and Gone.

Individual	Unit	Group	Team
Rover Zip Rover Heads and Zip	Rover In Rover Out Rover Stack	*Any Rover Unit stunt used in conjunction with one other unit that is also stunting.	Blast Right Blast Left Dogs Blitzes All

*Combinations are too numerous to list, refer to the Stunts.

Table V Weak Outside Linebacker Stunts—Rover

2. Under and Over Defenses. Rover plays the same as in Pro defense.
3. "50" Defense. Rover plays in the "Red" position. (See secondary section)
4. Seventy and Nose Defenses. Rover plays as in split defense.
G. Basic Rover Pass Coverage Techniques (Blue Alignment).
   1. Pass Keys: Rover keys the tackle, near back, and the quarterback.
   2. Responsibilities: Against drop back action Rover reacts out and back (45 degrees). Rover must always be alert to help on the Look-In Pass. First, take away the Look-In Pass, then cover the flare. Do not react forward until the ball is in the air. If a screen develops, get into it as quickly as possible, knifing through the blockers.

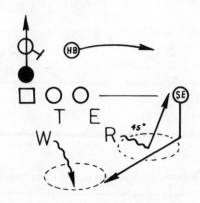

a) Correct

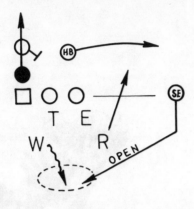

b) Incorrect

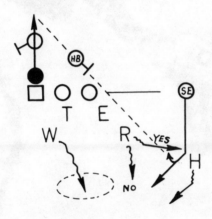

c) When back blocks

Figure 178a, b and c Rover's Correct and Incorrect Way of Covering the Look-In, the Flare Pass, and the flat area.

    a. If a back releases, keep leverage on him. Remember that on inside stunts, you have no inside help from the linebackers.

    b. If back blocks, react out and back at 45°. Take an interception route across the face of the Split End. Expect the Hook, Sideline or Curl route by the Split End.

    c. If the backs flow away, cushion back and cut off the throw back pass to the Split End. Check for a counter or reverse play as you go.

NOTE: For Rover's responsibilities in various secondary coverages, see Secondary Coverage Play.

HOW TO COACH SPLIT-PRO SECONDARY PASS COVERAGE PROCEDURES AND TECHNIQUES (ROVER, HOUNDS AND FOX)

7

In the Split Pro Secondary, the ability to play man-to-man is preferred even though zone coverage can be used successfully. Speed, quickness, and the ability to react correctly to a thrown ball are three of the first requirements of the defensive halfbacks and the safety.

The safety should possess more speed than the halfbacks because he is asked to be the outfielder and catch any breakthrough from sideline to sideline.

A. General Concept

Due to the alignment and philosophy of the Split-Pro defense, more man-to-man coverage is used than zone coverage.

This may sound risky, but with added pressure up front, complimented with various combinations of man coverage (combination man-and-zone, bump-and-go-man) and secondary stunting, it makes it very hard for the quarterback to read and throw well balanced.

The author cannot emphasize enough the importance of stunting (or moving late) into various coverages and attacking key receivers when playing a team with an outstanding passing attack. Move the secondary from one alignment to another and camouflage the coverages until the last possible moment. Instead of lining up in double coverage, stunt into it on a predetermined key. The same goes for the other secondary tactics described later in this chapter.

On the next few pages, you will find techniques on man and zone coverage, special man-to-man tips, and a number of team coverages that will give added variation and cause the passing teams some problems.

135

If added security is needed against the passing game, Mike can check-pro and the secondary can use a pure zone type of coverage from a three or four-deep alignment. By bringing the Rover back into the free safety spot, one can employ the four-deep principles.

In this system of defenses it is very important that potential pass receivers trying to release through the line are clotheslined or detained by the linebackers as much as possible. All linebackers are instructed to knock down any and all receivers if they threaten their zones (practice time must be devoted to this phase of the game). The defensive backs must also master the techniques of bump and recover and stunting if maximum protection is to be maintained.

Most of the coverages from the split and pro defenses incorporate the following principles:

1. Detain potential receivers at the line of scrimmage.
2. Cause congestion at the line so backs cannot release free.
3. Continuously pressure the passer so that he *must* throw quickly.
4. Vary the pass rush and force the offensive line to use more than one method of protecting the passer. Do not give the line a predictable pattern that requires no change in blocking assignments.
5. Vary the coverages so that the quarterback cannot read consistently. Make the quarterback read the coverage after the snap of the ball —not before.
6. Knock potential receivers around before the pass is released, thereby disrupting their routes and timing.
7. Play the down and situation tendencies.
8. Punish the receivers if they catch the ball.

B. Secondary Huddle and Post Huddle Procedures

Everything starts in the defensive huddle. After the Mike linebacker makes the defensive front call, the safety will make a color call (for personnel placement) and a coverage call (gives the secondary the types of techniques to be used in covering their receivers). After the huddle break, the defensive halfbacks, safety and the Rover will align in their post huddle positions and proceed as follows.

1. Read the Offensive Huddle Break. In order to locate specific keys and recognize the formation as quickly as possible the halfback, safety, and Rover should read the offensive huddle break.
2. Move to the Correct Position. Once the offensive alignment is recognized, the secondary personnel should move quickly to their correct positions. In doing so they should review mentally their assignments and concentrate on their assigned keys. (Analyze vertical and lateral field position)
3. Concentrate Hard on Assigned Keys. Regardless of the coverage

call, the secondary will have focal points or specific keys. At the snap of the ball, their keys will tell them whether it is a pass or a run.

C. Secondary Alignments (Color Calls)

Personnel alignments in the secondary are designated by the use of colors. The color called tells the Rover and Safety where to line up against the offensive sets. The halfbacks remain the same; and unless they are told otherwise, they will always go to the outside zone or man. This type of alignment system enables the coach to align and match up the personnel according to ability, thus avoiding a physical mismatch.

The secondary alignments and coverages, like the various stunts listed for the front personnel, are used only as personnel and the scouting reports dictate. It is possible and sometimes necessary to vary the over-all coverage from week to week. However, the basic alignment is "Blue."

1. The "Blue" Alignment. On a "Blue" call the Rover aligns on the split end side of the formation and in the flat area, the safety (fox) aligns in the middle of the field, and halfbacks (Hounds) align on their side of the field.

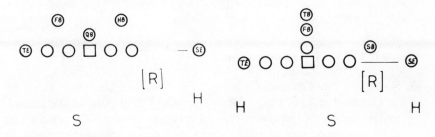

a) Pro Formation   *b) Slot Formation*

Figure 179a and b The "Blue" Alignment

2. The "Red" Alignment (Monster Type Secondary). On a "Red" call the Rover aligns on the flanker and slot side of the formation in the flat area, the safety aligns in the middle area, and the halfbacks align on their respective sides of the field.

a) Pro Formation

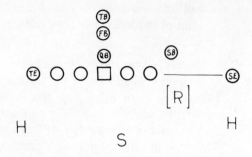

b) Slot Formation

Figure 180a and b The "Red" Alignment

3. The "Gold" Alignment. On a "Gold" call the safety aligns in front of the tight end, the Rover aligns in front of the remaining halfback, and the halfbacks align on their respective sides of the field.

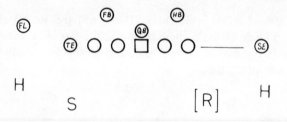

Figure 181 The "Gold" Alignment

D. Secondary Pass Coverage Calls

The color call of "Blue," "Red," or "Gold" will position the secondary personnel for about any type of coverage desired. The selection of alignments to be used should be based upon personnel available and conference offensive trends. After the color call the safety will give a coverage call which tells the secondary defenders what type of techniques are to be used in covering the receivers.

1. The "Man" Call. On a "Man" call the defenders align in their designated areas (as directed by the color call) and move late to a position over the man they are assigned to cover. On a "Man" call, basic man-to-man techniques are used. To vary the type of man techniques, an additional word can be added such as "Tight," "Loose," or "Inside."

a. Basic Man-to-Man. This type of coverage is used most of the time. The halfbacks align approximately six yards deep and on the outside shoulder of the receiver. When the receiver releases, the defender lets him close the gap to within three yards (referred to as the "Pad") and plays him from there.

b. Tight Man-to-Man. This type of man coverage is used with team stunts or on the goal line. The halfbacks move late to a position four or five yards deep and cover the receivers real tough.

The idea is to definitely take away any route less than ten to twelve yards deep. Here we plan on the stunters getting to the quarterback or forcing him to throw the football before the receivers can cover more than 15-20 yards. If a coach adopts this theory, he should use a special drill for the secondary defenders that is called a butt-to-butt drill.

In the butt-to-butt drill the receiver positions himself in back of the defender and facing downfield. The defender is now positioned behind him butt-to-butt. On a signal from the coach, the receiver sprints off on his route and the defender spins and chases him as if he is beat deep. As they proceed down the field the defender keys the receiver's helmet. When the receiver turns to look for the ball, the defender cuts in front and goes for the interception. After a few weeks of this drill, one will be surprised how well the defenders can recover and either knock the ball down or make the interception.

One additional coaching point here is to have the rest of the team yell "Ball" when the ball is released to inform the chaser that the ball is on its way. (Use the same call in a ball game.)

c. Loose Man-to-Man. Sometimes a loose type of man coverage is handy in prevent and long-yardage situations. On a "Loose" call, the defensive halfbacks loosen up to a position of seven or eight yards deep and play for the bomb first and the short pass second, remembering that they will have help from the linebackers on the underneath routes.

d. Inside Man-to-Man. On an "Inside" call the defensive halfbacks align on the inside of the outside receivers and about four or five yards deep. They face 45 degrees toward the receivers and take away any inside route, using the sideline as an outside defender. This type of man coverage is also used on the goal line, but the distance is cut down in relation to the distance to go for the touchdown.

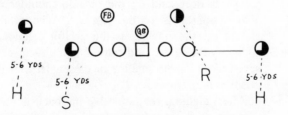

a) Basic Man-to-Man

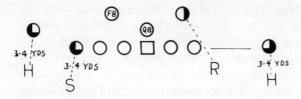

b) Tight Man-to-Man

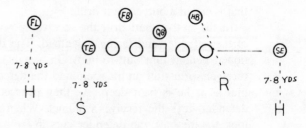

c) Loose Man-to-Man

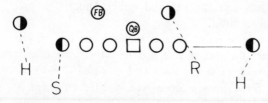

d) Inside Man-to-Man

Figure 182a, b, c, and d Variations of "Man" Coverage

e. Techniques of Man-to-Man Coverage. In teaching "Man" coverage, start at the huddle. Before leaving the huddle, secondary personnel should be aware of the down and yardage needed for the first down. After the huddle break, they should read the offensive huddle for their keys and align quickly. For man coverage the secondary is instructed as follows:

1) In basic man coverage the halfbacks align approximately 45 degrees, facing inside toward the offensive set. They set up six yards deep and on the outside shoulder of the receiver, always conscious of the sideline. Whenever possible, they should use the sideline as the twelfth defender, and in doing so, apply the seven-yard rule: When a receiver splits to within seven yards of the sideline or closer, let him gain the outside position if he wants it.

After aligning, the defensive halfback is instructed to concentrate on the receiver by focusing the eyes on a chosen spot just at the base of the jersey numbers (providing that he is in the upright position). Defenders must learn to discipline themselves to the point that they can ignore everything but the receiver. It has been said that concentration is 75% of man-to-man coverage.

2) At the snap of the ball, square up (keeping the shoulders square to the line of scrimmage) and begin the backpedal, keeping the weight on the balls of the feet. Do not rock back on the heels. The body should be bent and balanced, with the arms hanging loosely and the feet approximately shoulder width during the initial backpedal stage. Avoid vigorous arm pumping, this will only slow down your reactions on fast cuts.

Also, keep the feet moving (running in place) and close to the ground at all times so that quick adjustments can be made without too much wasted motion. Keep the weight slightly forward.

3) Always maintain position on the receiver (outside shoulder). Never let him gain a head-up position. At a position no deeper than seven yards down field, position yourself three yards from him (referred to as the Final Pad). At all times keep the feet moving, pedal the feet regardless of how fast or slow the receiver is moving—even if the receiver is not moving.

Keep in mind that most receivers will make their cuts approximately ten yards from the line of scrimmage, and anticipate them. When the receiver shows a sign of slowing down or he straightens up, he will usually enter what we call a "faking stage." When this happens, the defender should stay low, get under control, and be ready to sprint once the final cut is made. (As a general rule, you can ignore the first fake.)

4) As the receiver makes his final break, react by stepping quickly with his break. Drive off hard with him, maintaining leverage on him so that he has to make contact with you in order to cut back.

After the receiver makes his break and you have made your drive, get in stride with him, step for step. Look for the ball through the receiver.

5) React to the ball. The first thought should be to intercept the football. If this is impossible, do the following—in this order:
   a) Knock the ball away from the receiver.
   b) Strip the receiver.
   c) Tackle the receiver, or (as a last resort if a touchdown is unavoidable) commit pass interference.

6) Always remember that:

a) The post route is the most dangerous route to defenders using man-to-man techniques. Anticipate an inside cut from your receiver on every play. If you do not have a free safety supporting you, cheat to a head-up position on the receiver. If you do have free safety help, work an outside and under (for sideline routes) or outside and over the top (for curl routes) maneuver with the safety.

b) Always collision receivers if the receiver has the edge or when you have help deep.

c) When playing a wide receiver inside the ten yard line (goal line defense), move to the receiver's inside shoulder and do not let him release to the inside.

d) If you are a step behind the receiver running a sideline route and the ball is thrown well, bat the ball down with near hand; and in the event of a completion, have the far arm ready to grab the receiver.

e) When playing through the receiver, always go high through the shoulders and head if the pass is high. If the pass is low, go through the small of the back.

f) When playing the receiver and ball, strive to do the following—in this order:
  1) Intercept the ball.
  2) Bat the ball down.
  3) Straighten the receiver's arms or bat the helmet.
  4) Punish the receiver—making the tackle.

g) If you arrive too late (ball gets to receiver before you do), always break down (good football position) 2½-3 yards from the receiver, let the receiver declare his direction, then make the tackle using correct angles and the sideline. Make the sure tackle, higher than usual.

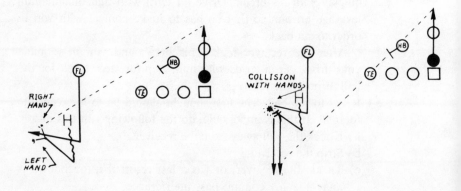

a) Playing the sideline route—Inside hand in position to bat the ball down and the outside hand in back of the receiver for the tackle in case of the reception.

b) Playing the sideline and go route—Collision the receiver with the hands pushing him off balance, then drive deep with him.

Figure 183a and b Man-to-man halfback techniques

2. The "Zone" Call. Two types of zone coverage are used in the Split-Pro defense. They are straight three-deep and roll zone. The rotation in a roll zone is designated by the use of numbers or a word.
   a. A "One-Zone." Provides rotation on only one action and that is play action—away from the Rover. On all other play actions, the secondary plays a true three-deep.
   b. A "Two-Zone." Provides secondary rotation on two types of play action: On play action away from the Rover and on drop-back action the secondary will roll strong. On play action toward the Rover, they will play a true three-deep. The "Two-Zone" is usually used when the wide side of the field is opposite the Rover's side.
   c. The "Three or Stay Zone" provides a true three deep with no rotation, regardless of play action.
   d. The "Four or Roll Zone" calls for secondary rotation toward backfield flow right and left.
   e. Techniques of Zone Coverage.
      In zone coverage the secondary personnel align in their assigned areas and key specific receivers and then the ball. They must learn to recognize the formations and the passing potential of each in order to pick up their keys quickly. Two basic keys are used in zone coverage. An initial key to determine whether it is a pass or a run, and a secondary key to determine when and where the ball will be thrown. The initial key is usually a receiver, while the secondary key is the ball and quarterback. For zone coverage the secondary is instructed as follows:
      1) Halfbacks align and locate their initial key quickly. Set up in a position seven yards deep and on the outside shoulder of the outside receiver with the outside foot back. Drop the hips by bending slightly at the knees and waist. When the receiver crosses the line of scrimmage, shuffle back and out a couple of steps. Play for a pass until your secondary key, which is the quarterback and the ball, indicates a run. The safety aligns in the middle of the field and keys through the interior

part of the line to the quarterback and the ball. At the snap the safety tries to get an overall picture of the action and then focuses in on the quarterback.

2) After the snap of the ball, both the halfbacks and the safety shuffle back a couple of steps looking for a pass. If the keys show a pass, move quickly to the middle of the zone. Make sure that you are at a point in your assigned zone that will enable you to cover all points in that zone equally well and as quickly as possible (at times we do not play a true zone; we allow the defenders to favor the receivers who enter their zones). Cushion back only as fast as the receivers move down field. This helps eliminate the gaps between the underneath and deep coverage. We prefer to expand as needed.

As a general rule, if a receiver is entering your zone, coming straight at you, do not let him close the gap to more than six yards. If the receiver is running a route parallel to the line of scrimmage, cut the pad to about four yards and keep the outside position on him. The distance between the passer and the receiver will also be an influencing factor. The greater the distance, the looser you can play.

3) As you move to your zone, focus in on the quarterback and the ball. Try to read his eyes, arms and head for a tip that may give away his intentions prematurely.

4) When the ball is released, sprint to a point that you can jump and intercept the ball at its highest point. Always intercept the ball at its highest point and think in terms of interceptions first. However, there are exceptions to this rule. If you cannot make the interception, knock the ball away from the receiver. If the receiver catches the ball and you are close to him, strip him of the ball. If the receiver has the ball, break down at two or three yards from him and make the sure tackle.

3. Combination Coverages. Special words are used to designate coverages involving both zone and man. Coverages involving attacking techniques are called the same way. (See a and b below.)

a. Gold, Free Man. Willie keys the halfback. If the halfback blocks, Willie is free to help as needed. Rover plays a free safety while the other backs cover man to man. Refer to "Team Coverages" for illustrations.

b. Blue, Solo Zone. The safety rolls both ways on flow. If flow is away from the halfback, the halfback picks up his receiver man-to-man. If flow is toward the halfback, he levels in the flat. Refer to "Team Coverages" for illustrations.

4. Coordinating Secondary and Underneath Pass Coverage.

Pass defense is a matter of angles. If the linebackers and secondary personnel move at the correct angles on the snap and adjust the angles as the receivers proceed down the field, the passing lanes will be closed. If defenders retreat at the right angles, the passer will have to throw the ball over outstretched hands to complete the pass; this is especially true on the look-in, curl, and post routes.

Playing the angles and obstructing the passing lanes is of prime importance in pass defense. The players must thoroughly understand these two principles if they are to function properly as a well-coordinated team.

If the defenders are centered and well-distributed within their passing lanes, the quarterback will have to lob the ball over and between the defenders in order to get it to a receiver. This, of course, gives the secondary defenders more time to react for the interception. The figures to follow will illustrate the various passing lanes as they correspond to the specific routes. Note the positions of key players in the passing lanes. They should be centered in the lane, well distributed in relationship with other defenders, and when the ball is thrown, reaching for the sky.

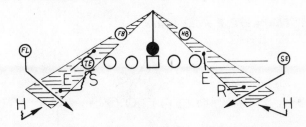

Figure 184 The "Look-In" Passing Lane

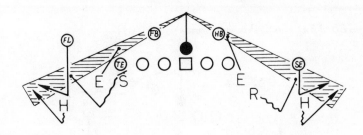

Figure 185 The "Side Line" Passing Lanes

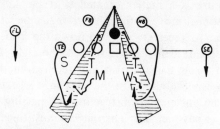

Figure 186 The "Hook" Passing Lanes

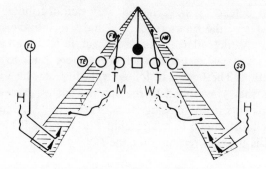

Figure 187 The "Curl" Passing Lanes

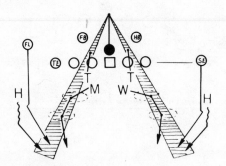

Figure 188 The "Post" Passing Lanes

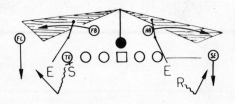

Figure 189 The "Flare" Passing Lanes

In order to guide the underneath defenders, calls are used. The calls are "Curl" and "Deep." When the linebackers hear these calls, they react accordingly. Although sometimes it is difficult to get players to make calls in game situations, they do serve a worthwhile purpose in practice. The coach can work each move as a separate technique since each one has a name.

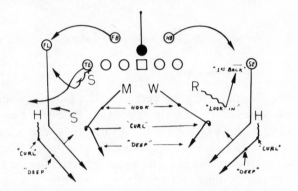

Figure 190 Coordinating Secondary and Underneath Coverage

a. Stopping the Look-In Pass. At the snap of the ball and the recognition of a pass, the ends rush the passer, keying the quarterback. When the quarterback sets up to throw, the ends get their hands high in the air to either bat down or deflect the ball. Rover's first reaction to a drop-back pass is to fade out and back obstructing the look-in passing lane. Sam detains the tight end; but as he does so, he should give ground back and outside until he is in the look-in lane.

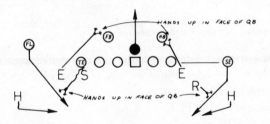

Figure 191 Stopping the Look-In Pass

b. Stopping the Curl. In order to throw the curl pass, the quarterback should be forced to throw over the out-stretched arms of the tackles and the linebackers. The linebackers, after checking the possibilities of a draw, screen and hook, move on out into the curl zones.

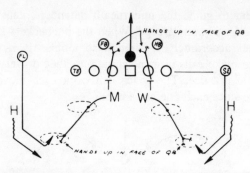

Figure 192 Stopping the Curl

c. Stopping the Post. The post route is a problem route, and its use has resulted in many touchdowns. Probably two of the most effective ways of playing the post route is with a free safety or a pure zone-type coverage. Another maneuver which helps is to keep inside leverage on the wide receivers; but, in turn, this also aids certain other routes.

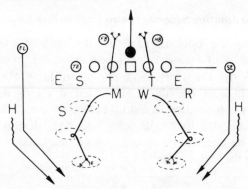

Figure 193 Stopping the Post Route

If good fast defensive halfbacks are available, it may be worthwhile to consider using an inside type of man coverage. (See Figure 182 d)

5. Individual Position Play.
   a. Halfback Play:
      1) Stance: Turn slightly (about 45 degrees) to the inside so that you can see formation out of the corner of the inside eye. Maintain a well-balanced stance so that you can move quickly and easily.
      2) Alignment: Take a position on the outside shoulder of the receiver, and about 5-6 yards from him (depends on his and your speed).

3) Assignment: On the snap of the ball, shift your key to the receiver's numbers (spot between the two numbers and at base of the numbers), square up and backpedal, keeping leverage on the receiver. Keep your feet moving continuously, regardless of the receiver's speed down the field. Maintain a pad of about three yards. Do not take fakes (ignore his first move); when the receiver cuts, shuffle step until his speed forces you to turn and run. Then get in stride with the receiver, playing for the interception.

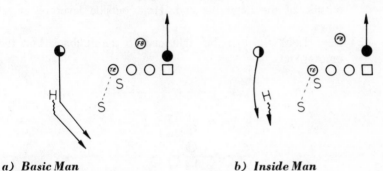

a) **Basic Man**   *b)* **Inside Man**

Figure 194a and b Halfback Leverage

4) Sideline Rule: If the receiver is six yards or less from the sideline, you can align on the inside and reverse your stance. Use the sideline as the twelfth defender.

C.P.: When the receiver drives deep, key his head—when he looks for the ball, you look. If he looks inside toward the field, do the same. If he looks toward the sideline, be ready to drive out and cut inside of him.

5) Special Calls.
  a) The "Crack" Call: If a flanker or split end takes the crack route, give the inside man (Safety, Rover, or Backer) the "Crack" call. Then support and contain the play as needed.

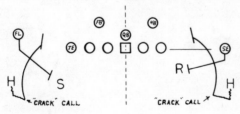

Figure 195 The "Crack" Call

b) When the ball is released toward fellow defenders, give a call of "ball, ball." If you hear a "ball, ball," call, do not touch the receiver because the ball is in the air.

c) When a run develops, make a "run, run" call. After a "run, run" call, let the receiver go and help support against the run.

  b. Safety Play (Blue Man):

    1) Stance: Can vary from square to staggered with the inside foot back (depends on the split of the flanker) looking to the inside.

    2) Alignment: Three to five yards deep and two to three yards outside of the defensive end. Hold outside leverage at all times.

    3) Key: Look through the tight end to the fullback and the quarterback.

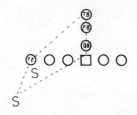

Figure 196 Safety Keys

    4) Assignment: Support on end runs and cover the tight end on passes man-to-man.

    5) Playing Techniques:

      a) Against a drop-back pass. Key through the tight end and cover him all the way man-to-man.

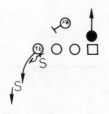

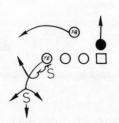

a) Correct—Keep outside lever-age and hold it.

b) Incorrect—He has two ways to go.

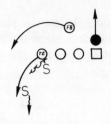
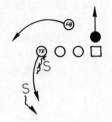

c) Incorrect—Facing Outside   *d) Correct—Facing Inside*

Figure 197 a, b, c, and d   Safety Basic Reactions

b) When the tight end releases on an outside route, shuffle through the slant area; you must give up outside leverage and roll with the receiver.

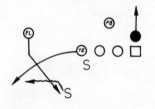

a) Correct—Quick Slant is cut off.   *b) Incorrect—Slant is open.*

Figure 198 a and b   Covering the Slant Pass

c) If the tight end blocks, shift key to the near back. If he blocks, you are free to help on flanker on inside routes. Sam will "Hold" the tight end man-to-man unless the near back releases. The Mike backer will also help on the delay routes.

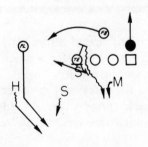
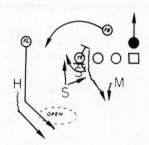

a) Correct   *b) Incorrect*

Figure 199 a and b   Tight End Delays

d) Action Pass:

[1] Action away. Get depth and help on the post throw back; then shift to the action. Sam takes the tight end throw back so that the safety may fall off and help as needed.

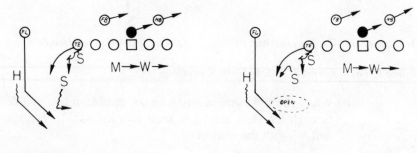

a) Correct   *b) Incorrect*

Figure 200a and b Flow Away

[2] Action your way. You have the tight end or support on runs.

6) Special Calls

a) The "Crack" Call. If a flanker takes a crack route on the safety, the halfback will yell "crack" and support on the run. See Figure 195.

b) The "I've Got Him" Call. The safety can release Sam of the tight end so that he can cover a halfback flare, safety just calls "I've got him."

c) A "Check-3" Call—Holds the secondary in deep thirds.

d) A "Check-Man" Call—Changes the coverage to "blue man."

e) The "You or Me" Calls—Indicate which player will cover the flat. Used on Cover-1 or Cover-2. Refer to the Coverage.

f) An "Easy" Call—Alerts the halfback of a possible switch. Also alerts Sam to go easy on the end for a quick read. (Delay of receiver delays switch call.)

g) A "Switch" Call—Confirms the actual switch of receivers between safety and halfback. (Apply the 8-yard rule; more than eight yards between receivers, "Easy" cannot be used.)

h) A "Plug" Call—Tells Sam that he is free to play the run. The safety will pick up the tight end without the usual delay by the Sam backer.

8 HOW TO COACH SPLIT-PRO SECONDARY TEAM COVERAGES

In this chapter you will find coverages of all types; each have their strengths and weaknesses. The reason for including a variety of coverages is to aid the coach in constructing tendency, formation, and opponent-personnel defenses.

Since tendencies, formations, and personnel will differ from game to game, it is essential that some of the coverages be altered in order to achieve maximum results. At times it may even be advantageous to add a specially designed coverage. A specially designed coverage may include a switch of defensive secondary personnel, man and zone combinations, attacking maneuvers that work on key receivers, secondary stunts or various types of double coverage.

A. General Concept.

The secondary coverages are divided into two basic groups—split-defense coverages and pro-defense coverages. Split-defense coverages include man, zone, combination man and zone, and special. Pro-defense coverages also include man, zone, combination man and zone, and special.

In the Split-Pro system the safety (Fox) calls the secondary coverage immediately after "Mike" makes the front call. The coverage called is determined by the front call, tactical situation, field position and opponent tendencies.

If the safety and the Mike linebacker are unable to master the art of manipulating the secondary and fronts according to the game plan, the coach should signal in the front calls and coverages from the sideline.

155

B. Split Defense Team Coverages.
  1. "Blue Roll" Coverage.
     a. Purpose: Used for tight formations (two tight ends and no flankers).
     b. Halfbacks: Halfbacks align seven yards deep and on the outside shoulder of the defensive ends. Assignments are as follows:
        1) Flow toward—level in the flat.
        2) Flow away—cushion deep 2/3 of the field.
        3) Drop—zone outside 1/3 of the field.
     c. Safety: Safety aligns 10-12 yards deep and over the offensive center. Assignments are as follows:
        1) Flow either way—go with the flow and take the outside 1/3 of the field toward flow.
        2) Drop—take deep middle 1/3 of the field.
     d. Sam and Rover:
        1) Flow toward—delay the receiver (tight end) and then force.
        2) Flow away—delay the receiver and then cushion back through the hook zone.
        3) Drop—bump the receiver (tight end) and then get into the flat zone.
     e. Mike and Willie.
        1) Flow toward:
           a) "Go" defense—Scrape
           b) "Read" defense—Shuffle down the line. Help in flat zone if back releases.
        2) Flow away:
           a) "Go" defense—Attack center and then go back to the hook zone.
           b) "Read" defense—Shuffle, check for counter and then go to the hook zone.
        3) Drop action—Go to the hook zone, then the curl zone, then the deep zone.

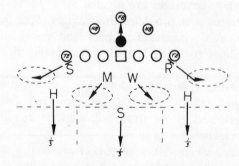

Figure 201 "Blue Roll" Coverage vs. a Drop Back Pass

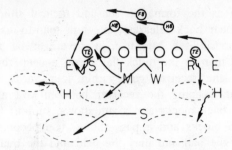

Figure 202 "Blue Roll" Coverage vs. the Sprint Pass

2. "Blue Man" Coverage.
   a. Halfbacks.
      1) Stance: Basic stance.
      2) Alignment: Against a tight formation align six or seven yards deep and two yards outside a normal end or wingback.
      3) Technique: Key your man and the ball hard. On the snap of the ball, square up and back-pedal, keying your man hard, but seeing the ball at the same time. When the receiver gets within three or four yards (varies according to the speed of the defender and receiver, adjust accordingly), get out of your back-pedal, turn, and sprint, keeping the the receiver between you and the ball. Do not let the receiver get too close to you.
      4) Responsibility: Man-to-man coverage; stay with your man wherever he goes. Do not get beat deep. If your man blocks, support against the run inside or outside as needed.
   b. Safety (Fox).
      1) Stance: Basic stance.
      2) Alignment: Always go to the tight-end side of the formation and take the tight end. Play five yards from the tight end and on his outside shoulder.
      3) Technique: Read the ball for flow. Key your man hard. At the snap back-pedal, being alert for the delay route. When the receiver gets within three or four yards of you, turn and sprint as fast as possible, keeping the receiver between you and the ball.
      4) Responsibility: Man-to-man coverage; if your man blocks, support against the run over the area where your man blocks. You must be alert for the delay routes and quick flat patterns by your receiver, but you cannot get beat deep.
   c. Rover.
      1) Stance: Basic stance.
      2) Alignment: Go to the split-end side of the formation and

align as the formation set and tactical situation dictate. If
the near back releases, take him man-to-man.

3) Responsibility: Man-to-man coverage; be ready to cover
   your man in the quick flat or on a deep route. Back-pedal
   until the receiver gets within four yards, then turn and
   sprint, keeping the receiver between you and the ball. If
   your back blocks and a run shows, support the run quickly.
   If he blocks and a pass shows, you become a free safety;
   read the ball and play the field and the quarterback's eyes.

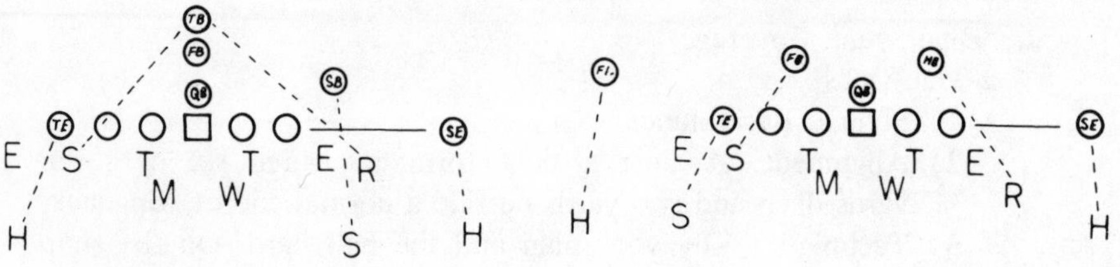

a) Slot Formation   *b) Pro Formation*

Figure 203a and b "Blue Man" Coverage

3. "Numbers" Coverage.

The underneath coverage can be varied to accommodate any
type of backfield set by simply using the numbers system. In the
numbers system each possible pass defender (underneath) is assigned a number. (See figure 204)

When a defender's number is called he will cover the first back
out on his side in case of a pass. All other front personnel carry
out regular defensive assignments without worry of pass coverage
responsibilities.

When using this type of coverage, Mike (the signal caller) will
make a two-digit number call. This call can be made in the huddle
or at the line of scrimmage (an automatic). Number calls should
be adjusted to match the offensive backfield set and lateral field
position.

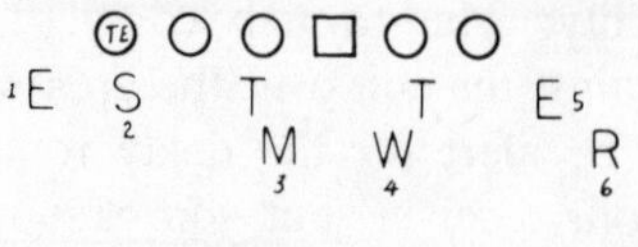

Figure 204 Personnel Number Designation

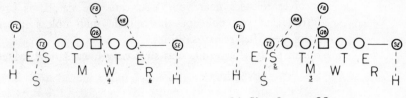

a) Numbers—46   b) Numbers—23

Figure 205a and b "Numbers" Coverage

4. "Blue Check-3" Coverage.
   a. General Concept: When "Check-3" is called, the defensive sec-
      ondary will play the three deep zones regardless of flow (play)
      action.
   b. Purpose: Used with both "split" and "Pro" defenses or when
      motion puts defender in both flats.
   c. Halfbacks: Zone outside 1/3 of the field.
   d. Safety: Zone middle 1/3 of the field.
   e. Rover: Zone onside flat area.
   f. Sam: Zone onside flat area.

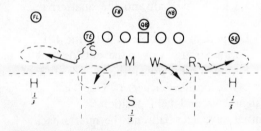

Figure 206 "Blue Check-Three" Coverage

5. "Blue-Zone, Cover-1"
   a. General Concept: Cover-1 is zone coverage with rotation only
      if sprint (or play action) is to the strong side. Backside half-
      back must play a tight zone or man on action #3. (See Figure
      207)
   b. Purpose: Insures split-end side flat, but is weak in the strong
      side flat on a drop-back pass. Used mostly when wide side of
      the field is toward the Rover.
   c. Strong-side halfback:
      1) Initial key: The ball and the quarterback.
      2) Action:
         a) Drop: Play a hard zone.
         b) Sprint toward: Take onside flat, use freeze, hammer, or
            slam techniques (See Attacking Techniques) if outside

receiver releases near you. You zone the flat. It is preferred that you collision the outside man unless it impairs your flat responsibilities.

c) Sprint away: Play zone and shift *easy* toward flow, watch for the throwbacks.

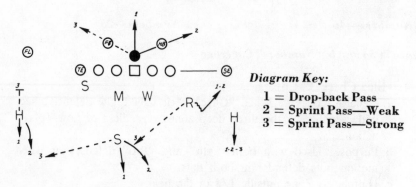

Diagram Key:

1 = Drop-back Pass
2 = Sprint Pass—Weak
3 = Sprint Pass—Strong

Figure 207 "Blue-Zone, Cover-1"

d. Safety (Fox):
  1) Initial key: The ball and the quarterback.
  2) Action:
     a) Drop: Cover middle 1/3 of the field.
     b) Sprint Strong: Cover the outside 1/3 of the field.
     c) Sprint Weak: Cover the middle 1/3 of the field.
e. Rover: Give onside backer a "One" call and loosen according to assignments and field position.
  1) Initial key: The ball and the quarterback.
  2) Action:
     a) Drop: Cover the onside flat.
     b) Sprint toward: Cover the onside flat.
     c) Sprint away: Cover the middle 1/3 of the field; look for the tight end deep (Sam will delay him).
  f. Weakside Halfback:
  1) Initial key: The ball and the quarterback.
  2) Action:
     a) Drop: Cover the outside 1/3 of the field.
     b) Sprint toward: Cover the outside 1/3 of the field.
     c) Sprint away: Use hard zone techniques.
g. Inside Linebackers: Use regular rules for "Read" and "Go" pass coverages. On Cover-1, the backside linebacker (Willie) must be alert for the halfback out when flow is away.
h. Field Position: Cover-1 is used mostly when in mid-field or when split end is to the wide side of the field.

6. "Blue-Zone, Cover-2"

    a. General Concept: Cover-2 is zone coverage with rotation toward the strong side on both sprint action away from the split end and on a drop back.

    b. Purpose: Insures the strong side flat. Used mostly when wide side of the field is away from the Rover.

    c. Strongside Halfback:

        1) Initial key: The ball and the quarterback.

        2) Action:

            a) Drop: Take the flat; use freeze, hammer, or slam techniques (See Attacking Techniques) if outside receiver releases near you. It is preferred that you collision the outside man unless it impairs your flat responsibilities.

            b) Sprint toward: Same as above.

            c) Sprint away: Play zone and shift *easy* toward the flow. Watch for a throwback.

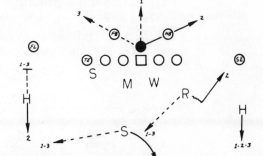

Diagram Key:

1 = Drop-back Pass
2 = Sprint Pass—Weak
3 = Sprint Pass—Strong

Figure 208 "Blue-Zone, Cover-2"

    d. Safety (Fox):

        1) Initial key: The ball and the quarterback.

        2) Action:

            a) Drop: Cover the strong side 1/3 of the field.

            b) Sprint strong: Cover the strong side 1/3 of the field.

            c) Sprint weak: Cover the middle 1/3 of the field.

    e. Rover: Give onside backer a "Two" call and loosen according to assignments.

        1) Initial key: The ball and the quarterback.

        2) Action:

            a) Drop: Cover the middle 1/3 of the field. Look for the tight end deep (Sam will delay him).

            b) Sprint toward: Zone the flat area.

            c) Sprint away: Cover the middle 1/3 of the field. Look for the tight end (Sam will delay him).

f. Weakside Halfback.
   1) Initial key: The ball and the quarterback.
   2) Action:
      a) Drop: Play a tight zone or man.
      b) Sprint toward: Cover the outside 1/3 of the field.
      c) Sprint away: Play a hard zone or man.
g. Inside Linebackers: Use regular rules for "Read" and "Go" pass coverages. On Cover-2, the backside linebacker (Willie) must be alert for the halfback out when flow is away and on a dropback.
h. Field Position: Cover-2 is used mostly when the wide side of the field is away from the split receiver.
i. Secondary "You-Me" Principles for Cover-1 and Cover-2.
   1) General Concept. The "You" and "Me" calls are used by the safety to designate who will roll into the flat. The man going into the flat should use attacking techniques whenever receivers are in his path or cross his path.

      These calls are used with covers one and two. On a "Me" call the safety rolls into the flat. (Cheat toward the assigned area.) On a "You" call the strong side halfback takes the flat.

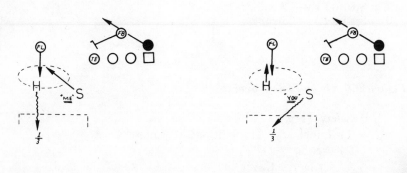

a) "Me"   *b) "You"*

Figure 209a and b "Me" and "You" Calls by the Safety

   2) Purpose: The ability to place the safety or the halfback in the flat or deep 1/3 helps to hide the poor defender, thus making it hard for the offense to pick on personnel. This also changes the "Read" for the quarterback. The two actions are needed to cope with various routes, and provide an effective way of playing offensive tendencies, favorite receivers, specific routes, and field position.

Coaching points for "You" and "Me" Calls (Base choice on key receiver's tendencies).

OPPONENT'S STRENGTH	CORRECT CALLS
1. Good "Look-In" Pass	Use "Me" Call
2. Good "Out or Sideline" Pass	Use "You" Call
3. Good "Post" Route	Use "You" Call
4. Good "Curl" Route	Use "You" Call
5. Good "Go" Route	Use "You" Call
6. Good "Hitch"	Use "You" Call
7. Good "Quick Out" by Inside Receiver	Use "Me" Call
8. "Wide Sideline" by Inside Receiver	Use "You" Call

7. "Gold/Free-Man" Coverage
   a. Assignments:
      1) Halfbacks: Same as Blue Man
      2) Safety: Take the tight end man-to-man. The Rover and safety may switch assignments depending on scouting report.
      3) Rover: Play at the free safety spot.
      4) Sam: Pick up the first back out on your side.
      5) Willie: Pick up the first back out on your side.
   b. Purpose: Used mostly with "Pro" defense. However, it is possible to use this coverage with the split defense when the backs line up in an "I" set or a strong backfield set. (See Figure 210)

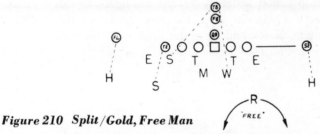

Figure 210   Split/Gold, Free Man

8. "Semi-Roll" Coverage (against a poor or slow tight end).
   a. Sam:
      1) On drop and sprint action toward—delay the receiver and cover the flat as the receiver threatens.
      2) On sprint action away—cushion for the throwback to the man you are over.
   b. Rover:
      1) Against a slot:
         a) On drop and sprint action toward—delay the receiver and cover the flat as receivers threaten.
         b) On sprint action away—cushion back for the throwback to the man you are over.

2) Against a split end: Align about two yards inside of the split end, at a depth of three or four yards (depends on his and your speed). You can also align in a heads position and shuffle back to a depth of four yards before the snap of the ball (must look inside).

    a) On drop and sprint away—stick with the split end man-to-man.

    b) On sprint toward—squat and attack the split man, then recover and play the flat as needed.

c. Halfbacks.

   1) Halfback on the split-end side.

    a) On drop and flow action toward—cover the outside 1/3 of the field.

    b) On sprint action away—shuffle toward flow and zone ½ of the field.

   2) Halfback on the tight-end side.

    a) On drop and flow toward—squat and force the receivers to the inside, taking all outside routes away from him. (Can use freeze techniques.)

    b) On sprint away—play the outside 1/3 for the throwback.

d. Safety.

   1) On flow action toward the split-end side—play the middle 1/3 of the field.

   2) On drop action and flow toward the tight-end side—shuffle and zone ½ of the field. Keep in mind that the halfback will squat, attack and force the receiver to the inside.

e. Linebackers. Can use "Go" or "Read" techniques.

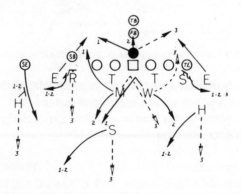

Figure 211 "Semi-Roll" Coverage

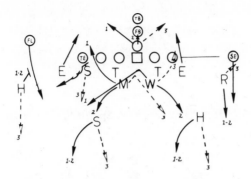

Figure 212 "Semi-Roll" Coverage vs. Two Wide Outs

9. "Single Man" Coverage
   a. Sam and Rover. (Can use "In" or "Out" stunts with the ends)
      Key to this coverage is based on the ability to pull up the quar-
      terback with Rover and Sam.
      1) Dropback pass—delay receiver and then cover the flat as
         it is threatened.
      2) Sprint toward—all-out rush.
      3) Sprint away—cushion back, you have the tight end or slot
         man-to-man.
   b. Inside Linebackers (use basic "Read" techniques).
      1) Onside backer—slide along the line as quarterback sprints,
         drop when quarterback sets up or throws back.
      2) Backside backer—check counter over center then cushion
         back and down the middle of the field.
      3) On dropback pass—execute read techniques.
   c. Ends (may use the "In" or "Out" stunt with Rover or Sam).
      1) On dropback and flow toward—execute an all-out rush.
      2) On flow away—trail hard.
   d. Safety. Align in the deep middle between the two inside receiv-
      ers, play deeper than usual.
      1) Flow either way—roll, playing zone, then man.
      2) Drop back—play middle 1/3 of the field.
   e. Halfbacks.
      1) Sprint toward—level in the flat. As you level, always col-
         lision any receiver in your path.
      2) Drop back—hard zone 1/3 of the field.

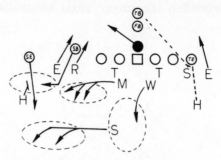

Figure 213 "Single Man" Coverage vs. Sprint Strong from a Slot Formation

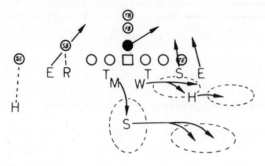

Figure 214 "Single Man" Coverage vs. Sprint to the Tight-End Side from a Slot Formation

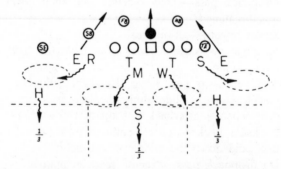

Figure 215 "Single Man" Coverage vs. Drop Back from a Slot Formation

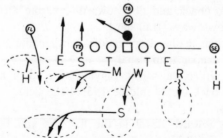

Figure 216 "Single Man" Coverage vs. Sprint Strong from a Pro "I" Formation

166

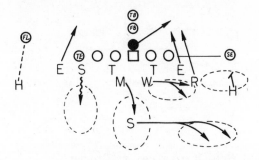

Figure 217 "Single Man" Coverage vs. Sprint Weak from a Pro "I"
Formation

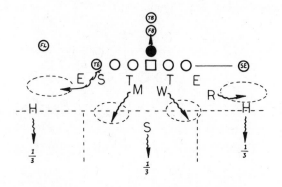

Figure 218 "Single Man" Coverage vs. a Drop-back Pass from a Pro "I"
Formation

C. Pro-Defense Team Coverages.

   1. "Pro/Gold, Strong Zone": On the snap, the secondary rolls strong,
using zone techniques. (See Figure 219)

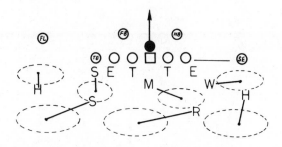

Figure 219 "Pro/Gold, Strong Zone" vs. Pro Set

   2. "Pro/Gold, Weak Zone": On the snap, the secondary rolls weak,
using zone techniques. (See Figure 220)

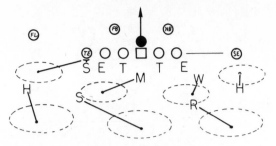

Figure 220 "Pro/Gold, Weak Zone" vs. Pro Set

3. "Pro/Blue, Check-3": On "Pro/Blue" Willie aligns in the flat on the flanker side. (See Figure 221)

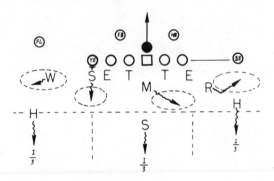

Figure 221 Pro-Defense with Check-3 Call

4. "Pro-Blue Heads, Check-3." On Pro-Blue Willie goes away from the split end side and works the flat area. If "Heads" is added to the defensive call, Willie works over the flanker. (See Figure 222.)

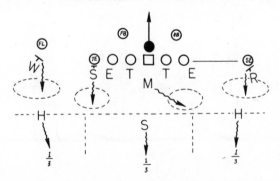

Figure 222 Pro-Defense with Heads and a Check-3 Call

5. "Pro/Gold, Free Man": On a "Gold" call the Rover and the safety can switch assignments depending on the scouting report. If the

tight end is slow and the weak back and split end are threats, a switch may be in order. (See Figure 223.)

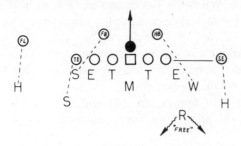

Figure 223 Pro-Defense with "Free Man" Coverage

D. Covering Motion.

Motion always causes problems for the secondary and underneath coverage. It cannot be ignored (providing the offense uses it properly); some adjustment must be made, and it must be sound or your opponents will out-flank you or align their best receiver on your poorest defender. Some teams require little or no adjustment because their motion fails to create an advantage.

A team should have more than one way of coping with motion. The method used will depend upon what type of motion is being used. Motion can be slow, fast, short, long, involving the slot, wing, or one of the remaining backs.

If a slot or wing is put into motion, it can easily be adjusted to by the secondary. If one of the remaining backs go in motion, it may force an interior adjustment with one of the inside linebackers. Naturally, you want to avoid a big change of assignment, and also not allow them to get a one-on-one mismatch. Figure 224 illustrates one way to cope with fast tailback motion.

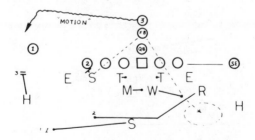

Figure 224 Covering Motion with a "Check-Pro and Roll"

When motion starts, Willie will "Check-Pro." When the call sounds, the tackles will move in slightly and expect the trap or fullback quick blast up the middle. Willie will move back into the Rover spot. If a pass develops, he will head for the curl area and then deep on the split-end side. When the Rover sees motion, he will yell "Willie" and head for the middle 1/3 looking for the number-two receiver on the strong side in case of a quick middle route. The safety (Fox) and halfback will roll toward the motion using the slam or hammer techniques on the number-one, outside receiver. The halfback will fall off to pick up the motion man.

If motion goes toward the split end, the Rover can pick him up and Willie will help in the hook and curl area.

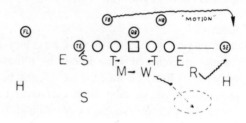

Figure 225 Motion Toward the Split End

The second way motion can be handled is by having Willie going man-to-man with the motion man. If slow motion is used, it is sound; if fast motion is used, it may require too quick a change and may be impractical. To avoid the perplexing problem of the backer covering the back down the sideline, a "Check-3" adjustment can be made. When a "Check-3" call is made, the halfback takes the deep 1/3 and the backer covers in the flat. (See Figure 227.)

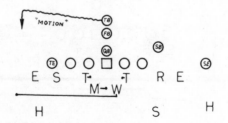

Figure 226 Man Coverage on Motion

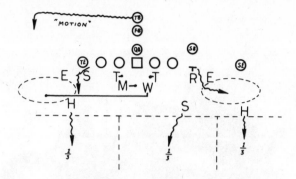

Figure 227 Coverage on Motion with "Check-3" Adjustment

The theory is this: Tackles tighten down and help the remaining backer plug the middle, the middle backer can then key the remaining back for dive, trap, or draw. Sam still delays the tight end and closes the off-tackle hole (no lead backs; therefore, Sam can delay rush on dropback passes, covering for onside end in case end loses contain on a scramble).

The strongside end (on the side of Sam) can give reckless rush inside or outside of the blockers on a pass because Sam will be able to cover for him.

HOW TO COACH SPLIT-PRO
9 SECONDARY STUNTS AND ATTACKING TECHNIQUES

As stated earlier in this book, secondary stunting and attacking maneuvers are the keys to stopping a good passer and pass receivers.

When the secondary moves and camouflages its coverages, it confuses the quarterback. When the defenders attack receivers, it disrupts the route timing and tests the receiver's mental and physical toughness.

Since most receivers are chosen for their ability to maneuver and catch the ball, they are unaccustomed to physical punishment. For this reason, they can be easily discouraged by attacking techniques.

A. General Concept.

Stunts in the secondary are divided into three categories: Individual Stunts that involve one secondary man, Unit Stunts involving two secondary men, and Team Stunts involving all eleven players.

Individual stunts can be called by designating the player involved: strong halfback, weak halfback, safety or the Rover. The effectiveness of secondary individual stunts depends upon the physical qualifications of personnel, field position, the tactical situation, and opponents tendencies.

B. Unit Stunts.

Unit stunts or maneuvers are those that involve more than one secondary man. These secondary unit stunts can be executed on the weak side or on the strong side of the offensive formation. In both cases defenders work as a team to destroy any possible reception. Types of Double Coverage in the Split-Pro are as follows (See Secondary Attacking Techniques):

1. Heads Coverage: In "Heads" coverage the defender aligns near the

173

receiver and detains the receiver by holding him up or forcing him into an inside or outside release.

2. Stunting Type of Double Coverage (Hammer, Slam, Freeze, and Cut): In the stunting type of double coverage the defender moves into position just before the snap and attacks the receiver on the snap of the ball.

C. Secondary Team Stunts.

Secondary team stunts are divided into two main categories: "Pressure" and "Defend."

1. Pressure Team Stunts. Pressure team stunts are the all-out blitzes. Everyone available rushes the passer, while the secondary covers, using tight man coverage. The secondary strives to make it impossible for the receivers to get open the first ten to fifteen yards, betting that the rush will smother the quarterback by that time.

2. Defending Team Stunts. Defending team stunts work just the opposite of pressure team stunts. This involves rushing with four and double covering (chop, cut, slam, hammer, freeze and delay) as many receivers (or favorite receivers) as possible.

C.P.: If the opponents have good protection or a good scrambling quarterback, thus making it hard to obtain a good rush, use a defending team stunt. If the opponents have poor protection, use the pressure team stunts.

D. Secondary Attacking Techniques (Bump-and-Go, Slam, Hammer, Cut and Freeze).

By incorporating attacking techniques and secondary stunts into secondary coverages, the passing game can be significantly limited. Nothing discourages receivers and passing quarterbacks more than to hold up and attack the receivers before they receive the ball. The temperament of a receiver can often be changed by attacking methods to the point that he will become completely ineffective.

Secondary personnel can hold up, knock around, control and sometimes even dominate receivers if proper skills and attitudes are drilled into them. Most defenders enjoy this type of play while the receivers dislike it very much. Outstanding success has been achieved with the following tactics:

1. The "Bump-and-Go" Technique.

a. The "Bump" is accomplished by attacking the receiver with a two-hand shiver or an arm and shoulder jolt. The blow is delivered with an upward motion into the pads or chest of a receiver to disrupt his direction of travel; thus, knocking him off his feet or at least off balance and out of his intended route path.

b. The recovery. After the bump the attacker must regain his original "Pad" and position so that he is ready to adjust to the receiver's move. The attacker must beat the receiver's recovery.

C.P.: These techniques cannot be used if the ball is in the air. Timing is extremely important. The blow must be delivered at a time when the receiver cannot avoid contact or effectively fight the jolt. The attacker must time the blow so that the receiver cannot avoid the contact and cannot regain his balance until the defender is balanced and in a position (with Pad) so he can adjust to the receiver's counter moves.

   2. The "Slam" Technique.
      a. Purpose. The "Slam" is a technique used by secondary defenders to delay and force an outside receiver to the outside and into the sideline (use against Hitch, look-in, wide receiver screens, and quick two- and four-step routes). The "Slam" technique can be used on the split-end side, strong side, or both at the same time.

C.P.: The "Slam" is most effective when the sideline is close enough that it can be used as an extra defender. If the receiver has a wide space between the defender and the sideline, it is difficult to corral him. (Most effective against a man on the line of scrimmage.)

      b. Alignment (Defender moves late to this position): Defender uses a two-point stance with the weight evenly distributed on both feet, and the body turned outside at a 45-degree angle on the inside shoulder of the receiver.

      c. Techniques: When the receiver moves, jolt and attack him using the bump-and-go, man-to-man technique. Stick to him like glue, forcing him outside into the sideline. If the receiver is down in a three-point stance, jolt his helmet with the heel of the outside hand and inside shoulder with the heel of the inside hand. Jab him again and again.

C.P.: When the defender jolts or bumps a receiver, he must recover and position himself before the receiver does.

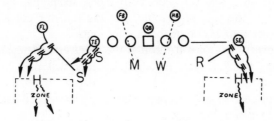

Figure 228 The "Slam" Technique

   3. The "Hammer" Techniques.
      a. Purpose. A technique used by the defender to delay and force an outside receiver to the inside or middle of the field. (Good against a sideline cut, Hitch, look-in, and other two- and three-step quick routes.) The "Hammer" technique can be used on

the split-end side, strong side, or both at the same time.

C.P.: Most effective when receiver has working room to his outside and away from the formation. This method forces the receiver back inside toward the formation, closing the distance between him, the safety and the linebackers.

    b. Alignment (Defender moves late to this position): Use a two-point stance, with the weight evenly distributed on both feet. The body should be turned inside at a 45-degree angle and on the outside shoulder of the receiver.

    c. Technique: When the receiver moves, jolt and attack him, using the bump-and-go, man-to-man techniques. Stick to him like glue, forcing him inside and toward the middle.

C.P.: Positioning and regaining balance is the key to all attacking techniques.

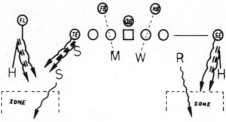

Figure 229 The "Hammer" Techniques

    4. The "Cut" Technique.

    a. Purpose. Used to cut receiver to the ground. This method is used to stop the super speed merchant who goes for the bomb and has the ability to out-maneuver the "Slam" and "Hammer" techniques.

    b. Technique. Use the side body-block technique at appropriate point in the receiver's route. Let the receiver come off the line and get into his route before the cut.

    c. Recovery. Try to roll through the receiver and regain your feet, zoning the flat area. Another defender will pick him up man-to-man.

C.P.: Use against a key receiver who has great speed and is a deep threat—the super star receiver.

    5. The "Freeze" Technique.

    a. Purpose. Used to attack a receiver at a specified point in his route (approximately four yards down field), knocking him off balance, delaying his cut, and destroying his timing with the quarterback.

    b. Technique. Take a position five yards down field in front of the receiver. When the ball is snapped, take one step back, and then come right up and take the receiver on just as hard as possible and try to knock him down. (Use a two hand shiver.)

c. Secondary Responsibilities. Recover as fast as possible and play the flat zone, picking up backs out or help on the man you hit if he takes a sideline route. You do not have to worry about deep routes; you have a man covering for you in the outside 1/3. Dominate the flat zone.

C.P.: This is a good technique to use against a fine sideline passer and receiver.

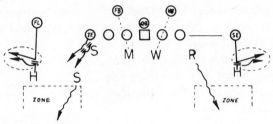

Figure 230 The "Freeze" Technique

6. The "Heads" Technique.

a. Normal Heads—line up head on receiver and hold him up.

b. Inside Heads—line up on the inside of receiver, delaying and forcing the receiver to the outside.

c. Outside Heads—line up on the outside of the receiver, delaying and forcing the receiver to the inside.

C.P.: Some receivers get wise to the "Heads" coverage techniques and become quite adept at faking and getting free. To counter these moves, the "Heads" man can align and move or shift from side to side.

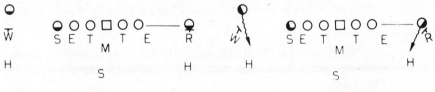

a) Normal "Heads"   *b) Outside "Heads"*

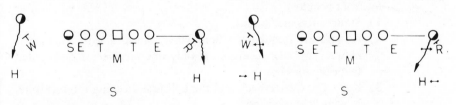

c) Inside "Heads"   *d) Fake*

Figure 231a, b, c, and d "Heads" Coverage

E. Defending Secondary Stunts: (Special coverage rules for "Slam," "Hammer," "Freeze," "Cut," "Dogs," and "Blitzes.")

   1. Calling the Stunting Coverages. The players named or numbered cover the two remaining backs out.

      a. 34 (Backers)/All Slam. Backers Mike and Willie cover backs out and the secondary uses "Slam" techniques.

      b. 15 (Ends)/All Slam. Ends right and left cover the backs out, and the secondary use "Slam" techniques.

      c. 26-Dog (Sam and Rover). Sam and Rover cover the backs out and the secondary use "Dog" coverage techniques (Blue Man).

   2. The last word or two words indicate the type and side that the secondary stunt is on.

      a. Weak—stunt is on the weak side.

      b. Strong—stunt is on the strong side.

      c. All—the same stunt on both sides.

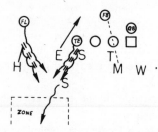 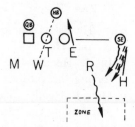

a) Strong "Hammer"   *b) Weak "Hammer"*

Figure 232a and b 34 (Backers) "Hammer" Stunt (Can be Weak, Strong or Both Sides)

   3. 34 (Backers)/All Slam (From Split-Blue Alignment): Inside coverage can vary on an "All Slam" Call—15 (Ends) and 34 (Backers).

      a. Halfbacks. (Can automatic to "Hammer" if needed; no change for front people.)

        1) Stance: Regular stance.

        2) Alignment: Regular position. Move late to a loose alignment between the two receivers. If only one receiver on your side, favor the outside.

        3) Key: The quarterback and the ball first, keeping the receivers in your field of vision.

        4) Assignment: Zone your area and hang until a man breaks clean, then pick him up. (See Figure 233.)

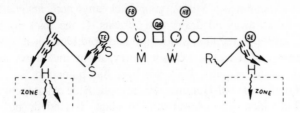

Figure 233 34 (Backers)/All Slam

b. Safety. (Can automatic to "Hammer" if needed.)
   1) Stance: Regular stance.
   2) Alignment: Regular position at huddle break, move late to a position on the inside shoulder of the outside receiver.
   3) Stance: Two-point, weight evenly distributed on both feet, turned outside at a 45-degree angle.
   4) Technique: On the snap of the ball, jolt and attack the receiver, bumping and riding him off the line and into the sideline. Use a bump-and-go, man-to-man until the whistle—stick to him like glue.

c. Rover. (Can automatic to "Hammer" if needed.)
   1) Stance: Regular stance.
   2) Alignment: In a "W" position or a position that you can reach the outside receiver before the ball is snapped.
   3) Assignment: Move late to a position on the inside shoulder of the outside man.
   4) Stance: Two-point stance, weight evenly distributed on both feet, turned outside at a 45-degree angle.
   5) Technique: On the snap of the ball, jolt the receiver, bumping and riding him off the line into the sideline. Use a bump-and-go, man-to-man until the whistle—stick to him.

d. Sam. (Slam and Hammer are the same to you; no change.)
   1) Stance: Regular stance on tight end.
   2) Alignment: Regular alignment and apply same rules.
   3) Assignment: On the snap of the ball jolt the tight end, bumping and riding him off the line to the outside. Stick with him anywhere he goes, man-to-man. If he tailors out, give switch call to the end and slightly favor the inside of him. Do not give him a choice of where he will release.

e. Inside Linebackers. (Slam and Hammer are the same to you; no change.)
   1) Stance: Regular stance.
   2) Alignment: Same as before. At the snap, move to a headup position on the onside back. If an "I" set, take the first back out on your side. Stay head up with your back.

3) Assignment: Mirror your back anywhere he goes, you must take away all draws and screens. If the back tries to release through the line, tackle him and hold him down.

f. Ends and Tackles. Do not worry about the draws and screens; just rush the quarterback and keep him pinned in.

4. 34 (Backers)/All Hammer (from Split-Blue Alignment).

a. Halfbacks (Can Automatic to slam if needed; no change for front people).

1) Stance: Regular stance.

2) Alignment: Take regular position at huddle break, then move late to a position on the outside shoulder of the outside receiver.

3) Stance: Two-point stance, weight evenly distributed on both feet, turned inside at a 45-degree angle.

4) Technique: On the snap of the ball, jolt and attack the receiver, bumping and riding him off the line and into the middle of the field. Use a bump-and-go, man-to-man until the whistle. Stick to him like glue.

b. Safety (Fox). (Can automatic to "Slam" if needed.)

1) Stance: Regular stance.

2) Alignment: Take regular position after the huddle break, then move late to a position between the two receivers. If only one receiver on your side, favor his inside.

3) Key: Key the quarterback and the ball first, but keep the receivers in the field of vision.

4) Assignment: Zone your area and hang until a man breaks clean, then pick him up.

c. Rover. (Can automatic to "Slam" if needed.)

1) Stance: Regular stance.

2) Alignment: Use "You Close" or the "L" position as they come up to the line of scrimmage. As the offense sets, move back into a halfback's position and play zone, favoring the inside of the receiver.

3) Key: Key the quarterback and the ball first, but keep the receivers in your field of vision.

4) Technique: Zone your area and hang until a man breaks loose, then pick him up.

d. Sam. (Slam and Hammer are the same to you.)

1) Stance: Regular stance on tight end.

2) Alignment: Regular alignment, and apply same rules.

3) Assignment: On the snap of the ball, jolt the tight end, bumping and riding him off the line to the outside. Stick with him anywhere he goes man-to-man. If he tailors out (splits out three to four yards), give a switch call and slightly favor

the inside of him. Do not give him a choice of where he will release.

e. Inside Linebackers. (Slam and Hammer are the same to you.)
   1) Stance: Regular stance.
   2) Alignment: Same as before. At the snap, move to a position head up on the outside back. If they are in an "I" set, take the first back out on your side. Stay head up with your back.
   3) Assignment: Mirror your back anywhere he goes, you must take away all draws and screens.
f. Ends and Tackles. Do not worry about the draws or screens Rush the quarterback and keep him pinned in.

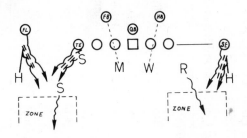

Figure 234 The 34 (Backers)/All Hammer Stunt—Team Alignments and Reactions

5. The 15 (Ends)/All Slam (Or Hammer) Stunt.
   a. Halfbacks. Can automatic to hammer if needed. Requires no change of assignments for the front people.
   b. Ends. Pick up the first back to release on your side.
   c. Linebackers. Mike and Willie can shoot the works (X or straight fire).

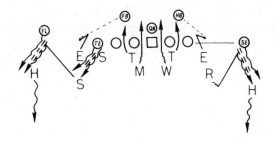

Figure 235 The 15 (Ends)/All Slam Stunt

For easy reference, all Secondary Stunts are listed by category in Table VI.

SECONDARY STUNTS (HALFBACKS, SAFETY AND LINEBACKER)

Variations of Basic Play: Man, Zone and Combination Man and Zone.

Position and Stunts

Halfbacks (Hounds)	Safety (Fox)	Rover	Willie
Zip	Zip	Zip	Zip
Heads	—	Heads	Heads
—	Slam	Slam	Slam
Hammer	—	—	—
Cut	Cut	Cut	Cut
Freeze	—	—	—

Team Stunts: Dogs, Blitzes and All Stunts

Table VI Secondary Stunts—Halfbacks, Safety, Rover and Willie

10 THE SPLIT-PRO
TEAM DEFENSES

The basic team defenses are divided into eight groups: basic defenses, basic mixers, short yardage defenses, pass rushing defenses, pass defending defenses, prevent defenses, automatic defenses, and goal line defenses.

These defenses are used as starting points in working out the defensive game plan. Variations, stunts, and coverages are added as needed from game to game. Refer to individual player technique sections for a complete list of variations and stunts.

A. The Split-Pro Basic Defensive Alignments.

On the following pages the reader will find a diagram of each basic defense against a dead "T" formation (no split ends or flankers). Also included are basic variations and basic stunts from each alignment.

The variations and stunts listed here may or may not adapt to the coach's present needs or personnel, even though they have been successful for us. If so, other adjustments, variations, and stunts can be found in the chapters on individual player techniques; adjust them accordingly.

1. "Split" Defense: (For individual player techniques and adjustments, refer to the proper chapter.)

a. Basic Alignment: (See Figure 236)

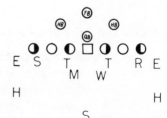

Figure 236 Basic Alignment

185

b. Possible Variations. The tempo of play can be regulated by using "Go," "Read," "Shoot," or "Loose" calls.

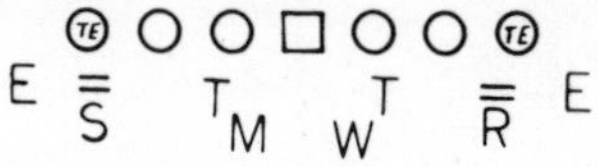

$$\overset{\circledR}{E} \overset{}{\underset{S}{\equiv}} O \ O \ \overset{}{\underset{M}{T}} \ \square \ \overset{}{\underset{W}{}} \ \overset{T}{\underset{R}{\equiv}} \ O \ O \ \overset{\circledR}{E}$$

Figure 237 "Split-Loose"

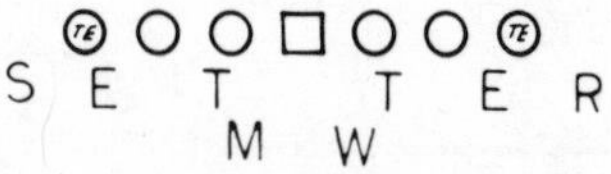

$$S \ \overset{\circledR}{E} \ O \ O \ \overset{}{\underset{M}{T}} \ \square \ \overset{}{\underset{W}{}} \ T \ O \ O \ \overset{\circledR}{E} \ R$$

Figure 238 "Split-Switch" (Exchanges outside linebackers and ends)

c. Possible Stunts: (Refer to chapters on individual player techniques for other stunts.)
   1) Tackles In—Backers Fire
   2) Tackles Out—Backers Fire
   3) Tackles Slant—Backers Fire (Liz–Rip)
   4) Sam and Rover In
   5) Sam and Rover Out (vs. Two Split End Formations)
2. "Pro" Defense (4–3 defense): (For techniques and adjustments refer to each chapter on individual techniques.)
   a. Basic Alignment. (See Figure 239)

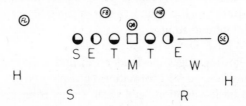

Figure 239 Pro Defense

b. Possible Variations. (Can use "Go," "Read," "Shoot," or a "Loose" type of play.) (See Figure 240)

$$\overset{\circledR}{E} \overset{}{\underset{S}{\equiv}} O \ O \ \overset{}{\underset{M}{T}} \ \square \ O \ O \ \overset{T}{\underset{\underset{W}{W}}{E}}$$

Figure 240 "Pro Sam Loose"

c. Possible Stunts (Refer to sections on position stunting.)
   1) Stunts from the "Pro" alignment are the same as from the "Split" alignment. Even though the stunters may start from a different alignment, they penetrate the same offensive gaps.

Some of the more effective stunts are: Pro-Willie and Sam Out, Pro-Tackles In—Backers Fire, Pro-Tacklers Out—Backers Fire, and Pro-Tackles Slant—Backers Fire (Liz–Rip).

2) Other Possible Stunts:

a) Deal Stunts between Mike and the tackles.

b) Almost all individual stunts.

3. "Tight" Defense (Wide Tackle-6 Defense). (For techniques and adjustments refer to each chapter on individual techniques.)

a. Basic Alignment. (See Figure 241)

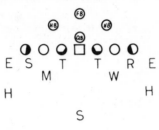

Figure 241 "Tight" Defense

b. Possible Variations: "Go," "Read" or "Shoot" type of play.

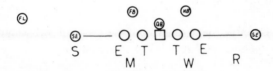

Figure 242 "Tight" (with Switches) vs. Two Split Ends

c. Possible Stunts (Refer to sections on stunts):

1) Some of the more effective stunts are:

a) Tight-Tackles In—Backers Fire,

b) Tight-Tackles Out—Backers Fire, and

c) Tight-Tackles Slant—Backers Fire (Liz-Rip).

2) Other Possible Stunts:

a) Sam and Rover "In" and "In Back" Stunts.

b) Deal stunts between the tackles and linebackers.

c) Blitz stunt—right or left.

d) Almost all individual stunts can be used.

4. Split-6 Defense. (For techniques and alignments refer to each chapter on individual techniques.)

a. Basic Alignment: Same as for split defense except that Sam plays tough in off-tackle hole with no pass responsibilities (can use switches if personnel so dictates). (See Figure 243.)

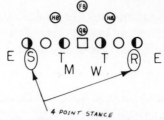

Figure 243 Split-6 Defense Basic Alignment (Sam and Rover can play up or down—no pass responsibilities)

b. Possible Stunts: Same Inside Stunts as in Split Defense.

B. Basic Mixers

1. "Wide" Defense. Sam and Rover move out to a head-up position on the ends.

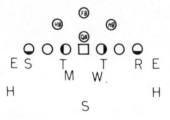

Figure 244 "Wide" Defense

2. "OH" Defense. Sam aligns on the nose of the center and plays "Read" techniques. Linebackers move outside.

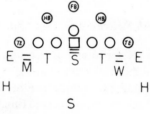

Figure 245 "OH" Defense

C.P.: This defensive alignment has been used effectively against the type of offensive set below.

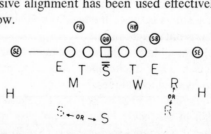

Figure 246 "OH" Defense vs. Two Split Ends

C. Short Yardage Defenses. In short yardage situations, another defender can be moved up into the line. This defender can be moved up on the line pre-snap or stunted into the line (can be one or more players) at the snap of the ball.

1. "Nose" Defense. Mike moves to a head-on, four-point position on the center. Willie stacks behind Mike.

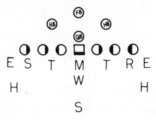

Figure 247 "Nose" Defense

2. "70" (Willie or Mike) Gap Defense. Willie or Mike takes the center-guard gap. Can stunt from this alignment, also. (See Inside Linebacker sections on stunting.)

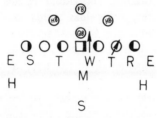

Figure 248 70-Willie Gap

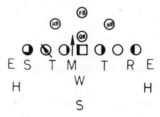

Figure 249 70-Mike Gap

3. Stunts. Various stunts can also be used as short yardage defenses. (See each section on stunting.)

D. Automatics. The automatics are used to adjust to an offensive change in alignment. Some of the automatics that are used from time to time are:

1. "Check-Pro." Used to change the Split alignment to the Pro defense alignment. This accommodates Spreads and Men in Motion.

  2. "Check-Strong." Used to adjust to a strong backfield set. Line-backers shift strong to compensate for offensive backfield set.

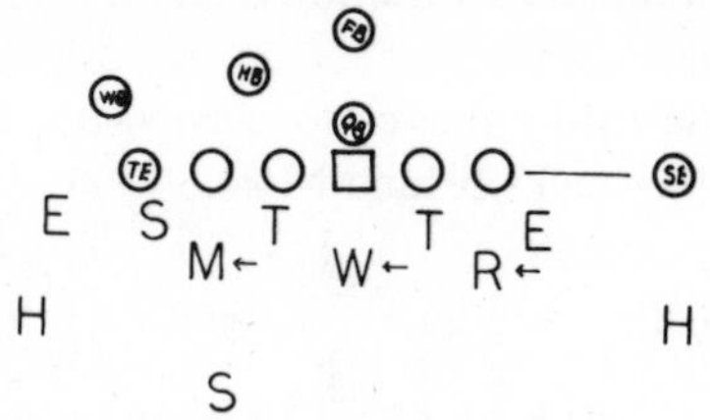

```
                        Ⓕ
               ⒽⒷ
         Ⓦ         Ⓠ
       ⓉⒺ  O  O  □  O  O ——— Ⓢⓔ
     E    S    T        T    E
           M←     W←     R←
       H                          H
             S
```

Figure 250 "Check-Strong"

  3. "Gap-Tackle." This call moves the tackle into the center and guard gap. Used at times to adjust to large splits. Linebacker also has option to shoot the gap if it is large enough.

  4. "One-Right" or "One-Left." This call moves the entire line one man to the right or left to accommodate unbalanced lines.

E. Pass Rushes. The pass rushes are divided into Individual, Unit, Group, Team (Dog and Blitzes), and "All" categories.

  1. Individual Pass Rushes. Individual rushes are the regular stunts like Zips and Fires. Individual stunts are used to attack specific personnel or weak areas in the pass protection.

  2. Unit Pass Rushes. Unit rushes are the regular unit stunts like "Back-ers Fire." Unit stunts are used to attack a two-gap area of the pass protection.

  3. Group Pass Rushes. Group rushes are the regular group stunts in-volving two units stunting at the same time like "Tackles In Fire." Group stunts will cover and attack a four-gap area.

  4. Team Pass Rushes. Team rushes can be of the six- or seven-man variety. The "Dogs" are the six-man rushes and "Blitzes" are the seven-man rushes.

  5. The "All" Pass Rushes. The "All" rushes are desperation rushes and will be classified in the blitz category.

F. Pressure Team Stunts.

  1. The Dog Stunts (Six-Man Rushes).

   a. Dog Rules:

    1) Secondary uses Blue-Man Coverage

    2) All players up front rush the passer (using dog rush tech-niques) unless their name or number is called. If their name or number is called they will pick up the first back out on their side man-to-man.

    3) Mike can call for a "Dog" in the huddle and automatic the rest of the call at the line of scrimmage after the backfield set forms (a "Two-Number" call).

4) Basic stunts can be used in coordination with the dogs. Example: "15-Dog, Tackles-In, Fire."

b. The "15-Dog (Ends)" Stunt.

1) Ends cover backs out if they release. Also motion.

2) Backers can run "X" stunt if wanted.

3) Secondary will use Blue-Man coverage.

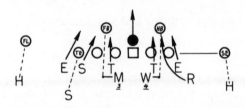

Figure 251 The "15-Dog (Ends)" Stunt

c. The "34-Dog" (Backers Mike and Willie) Stunt.

1) The inside linebackers tie up man-to-man on the backs.

2) The secondary will use Blue-Man coverage.

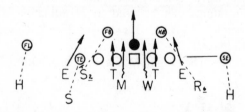

Figure 252 The "34-Dog" (Backers Mike and Willie) Stunt

d. The "26-Dog" (Sam and Rover) Stunt.

1) The inside backers can fire or use the "X" stunt.

2) Sam and Rover pick up backs man-to-man if they release.

3) The secondary will use Blue-Man coverage.

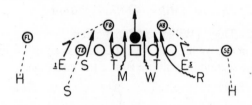

Figure 253 The "26-Dog" (Sam and Rover) Stunt

e. The "36-Dog" (Mike and Rover) Stunt.

1) Mike and Rover will cover the backs out of the backfield.

2) The secondary will use Blue-Man coverage.

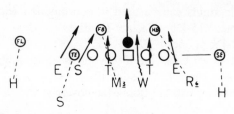

Figure 254 The "36-Dog" (Mike and Rover) Stunt

    f. The "24-Dog" (Willie and Sam) Stunt.
      1) Sam and Willie will cover the backs out of the backfield.
      2) The secondary will use Blue-Man coverage.

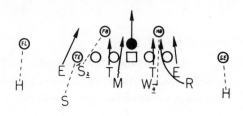

Figure 255 The "24-Dog" (Willie and Sam) Stunt

  2. The Blitz Stunts (Seven-Man Rushes).
    a. Blitz Rules:
      1) Secondary uses Blue-Man coverage.
      2) All players up front rush the passer (using blitz rush techniques) except for one player whose name or number is called. The one whose number is called will cover the back out on his side; or if he is located in the middle of the formation, he will pick up the first back out to either side.
      3) Mike can call for a "Blitz" in the huddle and automatic the rest of the call at the line of scrimmage after the backfield set forms (a "One number" call).
      4) Basic stunts can be used in coordination with the blitzes. Example: "2-Blitz, Tackles-In, Fire." (Used on the right hash mark.)
    b. Basic Blitzes. (See Figure 256 a, b, c, d, e, and f.)

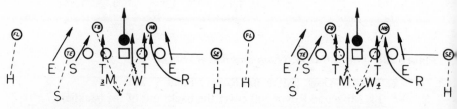

a) The 3-Blitz (Mike)   *b) The 4-Blitz (Willie)*

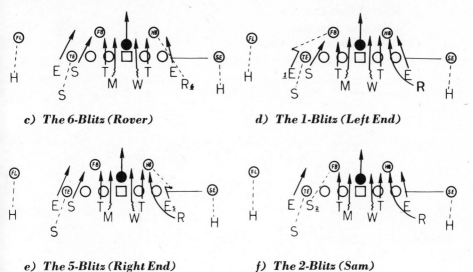

c) The 6-Blitz (Rover)   d) The 1-Blitz (Left End)

e) The 5-Blitz (Right End)   f) The 2-Blitz (Sam)

Figure 256a, b, c, d, e, and f Types of Blitzes

c. The "All" Blitz Stunt (Eight-Man Rushes).

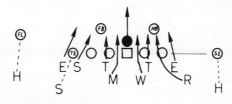

Figure 257 The "All" Blitz Stunt

G. Pass Defend.
   1. Concept.
      Sometimes it is tough to put on an effective rush because of good protection or a great scrambling quarterback. If a coach has to face one or the other, or both, it is wise to change up and defend as well as rush.

      The pass defend maneuvers are divided into three categories: Solid Defend, Stunting Defend and Prevent.
         a. The Solid Defend. The Solid Defend provides a defender in each and every zone, playing zone techniques.
         b. The Stunting Defend. The Stunting Defend calls for a four-man rush, while the secondary holds up the receivers or stunts into zones. (Combination man and zone coverages.)
         c. The Prevent Defend. The Prevent Defend calls for all-out defend, everyone playing loose, using zone techniques.

2. Solid Defend Defenses.
   a. Normal Situation:
      1) Huddle Call—Read
      2) Secondary Call—Blue Zone

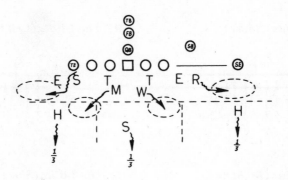

Figure 258 Split/Read, Blue Zone

b. Long Yardage:
   1) Huddle Call—Pro Read
   2) Secondary Call—Blue Zone

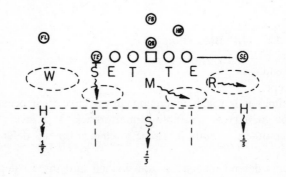

Figure 259 Pro/Read, Blue Zone

3. Stunting Defend.
   a. Pro/Read, Blue—Double Cut:
      1) Huddle Call—Pro Read
      2) Secondary Call—Blue "Double Cut."

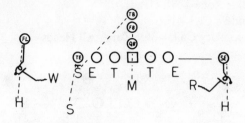

Figure 260 Pro/Read, Blue-Double Cut

b. Split/Backers All Hammer:
   1) Huddle Call—Split Read
   2) Secondary Call—Backers All Hammer

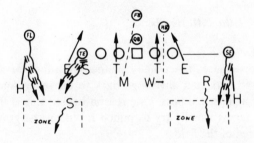

Figure 261 Split 34/(Backers) All Hammer

4. Prevent Defenses.
   a. Pro/Loose, All Zone
      1) Huddle Call—Pro-Loose and Read
      2) Secondary Call—All Zone

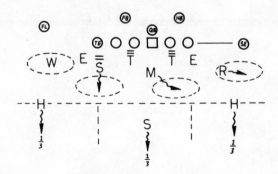

Figure 262 Pro/Loose, All Zone

b. Pro/Blue Zone—All Heads
   1) Huddle Call—Pro
   2) Secondary Call—Blue Zone, All Heads

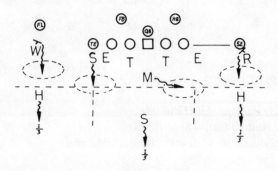

Figure 263 Pro/Blue, All Heads

H. Goal Line Defense.

Goal line defenses are usually of the seven-four or six-five variety. We have used both; but always go back to the seven-four, even though it is weaker against the pass. One reason behind this is that in our conference the teams usually try to punch it out on the ground when they reach this area of the field.

The Split defense is easily adjusted to the seven-four alignment by substituting a man (tackle for the safety) to play over the center and incorporating optional switches on both sides (due to personnel, we always used the switch) so that easy adjustments can be made to split ends, flankers and men in motion.

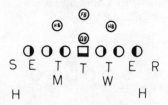

Figure 264 Seven-Four Goal Line Defense

In Table VII the reader will find a complete list of the basic team defenses within their own categories.

CATEGORIZED LIST OF BASIC DEFENSIVE ALIGNMENTS

Basic	Basic Mixers	Short Yardage	Pass Rushes
Split	Wide	Nose	Dogs
Pro	OH	70 Mike Gap	Blitzes
Tight	*Can also use stunts.	70 Willie Gap	*Basic middle stunts can be used also.
Split-6		*Can also use stunts.	

Defend	Prevent	Automatics	Goal Line
Split-Read	Split-Loose	Check-Pro	74 Goal Line
Pro-Read	Pro-Loose	Check-Strong	
	*Put in defensive backs for Willie and Sam	Gap-Tackle	
		One-Right	
		One-Left	

*Stunts could be used in some of the categories, but they are too numerous to list. Refer to the individual player sections and stunting.

Table VII List of Basic Defensive Alignments

11 HOW TO USE THE "SPLIT-PRO" DEFENSIVE SYSTEM

In discussing how to use the Split-Pro defensive system, it seems only right to start with the huddle and progress from there. Also included in this chapter are: how to call the defenses, defensive strategy, organizing the defensive battery, and special coaching points, problems, and remedies.

A. The Split-Pro Huddle Alignment.

1. The Huddle: The huddle is constructed as follows: (See Figure 265)

Figure 265 The Defensive Huddle

  a. The Front Row (two tackles and two ends):

    1) The right tackle will set up the huddle approximately two yards deep and slightly to the right of the football.

    2) The two tackles and the two ends assume a position with the feet shoulder width apart and parallel, with hands on knees and heads up looking at the Mike linebacker for instructions.

  b. The Second Row (Hounds, Fox, Sam, Rover, and Willie)

    1) Mike and the Safety (Fox) should be in a position so that they can see signals from the bench, if defenses are signaled from the sideline.

    2) The halfbacks (Hounds) should line up in the seam between the front row and the back row with hands on hips and heads up looking at the signal caller.

199

3) The safety, Sam, Rover, and Willie line up behind the front four with hands on hips and heads up looking at the signal caller.

2. The Huddle Procedure.

The signal caller (Mike) looks toward the sideline for instructions, then cups the hands around the mouth and calls the defense to the rest of the team.

The first call designates the basic defensive alignment. This is referred to as the front call. The front call can be "Split," "Pro," "Tight," "Over," "Under," "Wide," "Split-6," "50," "70 (Mike or or Willie)," or any other alignment designated.

After the front call is made, a second call is given that informs the front what type of play or stunt they are to use. This call can be "Go," "Read," "Shoot," or one of the many stunts listed in the text.

Once the front calls are completed, the Safety (after considering the defense called and the tactical situation) makes his calls. First an alignment call is made (a color) and then the coverage call.

After the calls are completed, both up front and in the secondary, Mike will then give the "Ready break" command. After the "Ready break" call everyone yells, "Hey!" claps the hands, and then hustles to the line to assume the post huddle alignment.

3. The Post Huddle Alignment.

At the line the tackles assume their positions (on one knee) on the line in a position where the offensive guards will be when they come to the line of scrimmage. The ends also assume a similar position outside the tackles and wait for the offense to arrive at the line. Sam will align over the ball but behind the tackles and read the offensive huddle break for the side he will align. Sam will go to the tight end side.

Mike and Willie will align just behind Sam and also read the huddle break. Rover will align behind the two inside backers and declare to the right or left side of the offensive set. The Fox and Hounds align in regular positions ready to expand to the offensive set in front of them. At this time, the Fox will make a final "check call" or "adjustment call" if it's needed to cope with special problems presented by the offensive set. (See Secondary Play.) Figure 266 shows the Post Huddle Alignment.

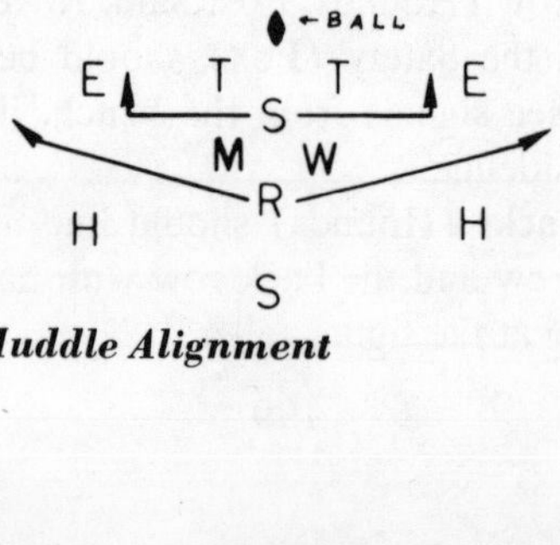

Figure 266 The Post Huddle Alignment

B. Defensive Strategy.

In setting up a defensive game plan, the coach must determine the strengths, weaknesses, and tendencies of the upcoming opponents. In doing so, many factors must be taken into consideration. For example, most offensive teams will develop certain offensive tendencies as the season progresses. These tendencies can be determined via films, the scouts, the computer, or from previous experience with the opponents. Some teams develop more tendencies than others, but even a few are helpful to the coach as he constructs the defensive game plan.

In some cases, two teams may use the same formations and plays. However, this does not necessarily mean that they are equally effective running through each hole along the line or passing into each possible pass zone. The determining factors in this case may be personnel.

Some teams on the schedule may use as many as four or five different offensive sets. If they are effective from each set, then the defensive coach may have to prepare special formation defenses, each designed to stop their most effective plays from each set.

Another factor that influences the defensive game plan is the defensive coach's own philosophy and background. Naturally, his trademark will be placed upon the defenses that he sets up. For example, where some coaches prefer to use an all-out rush against a good passer, others may prefer an all-out defend type of play and work for the interception. Here again, one's own personnel qualifications often determine the choice.

There are many other factors to consider, but in all cases it boils down to designing a set of defenses that will be effective against what has proven to be the opponents' tendencies and "bread and butter" plays.

In selecting defenses and special adjustments for the game plan, be sure that the players can handle the responsibilities assigned. For example, if you have big ends who lack speed, they will not be able to cover receivers out of the backfield. However, if you have a player (in any position) with exceptional qualities, it would be a mistake to limit his responsibilities. The alignments and the adjustments in themselves are not always the most important aspects—the determining factors are: how the alignments and adjustments are adapted to the personnel available and the situation in which they are used. This is the real criterion of any defensive game plan.

The following illustrates how the Split-Pro defense can be manipulated in order to cope with offensive tendencies and special alignments regardless of what they may be. The selection and the use of the stunts and adjustments to follow are determined by the offensive team's tendencies (Down, distance, etc.) and both teams' personnel. For diagrams of all stunts refer to each player's section. Other stunts not listed

A SPECIAL TENDENCY DEFENSE WITH A "BACKERS-FIRE" STUNT

"MIKE" (ROSS #54)

"BALL"

"WILLIE" (COTTRELL #43) IN "YOU CLOSE" POSITION

1

"MIKE" FIRES

"TACKLES" READ

"BALL"

"WILLIE" LOOPS INSIDE AND FIRES

2

Photos 1 through 4 illustrate the "Backer's Fire Stunt" from a specially constructed tendency defense. Willie (David Cottrell #43) is lined up in the "You Close" position (refer to Rover's alignments) and executes the "In" stunt from there. Mike (Jack Ross #54) who is lined up on the strong side shoulder of

the center also fires the center-guard gap. The tackles (Jack O'Donnell #77 and Leonard Henderson #61) use "Read" techniques looking for traps and off-tackle plays. Against this trap play from the "I" formation, the inside linebackers (Mike and Willie) come free and make the tackle for a three-yard loss. (Central State vs. Northeastern)

could be effective. The purpose of the material below is to stimulate the reader's thoughts pertaining to tendency defensing.

1. Sealing the Off-Tackle Hole. Use:
   a. "Split-Go" defense
   b. "Split/Tackles Read, Backers Go"
   c. "Split-Go/Sam Pinch"
   d. "Split-Go/Sam Zip"
   e. "Split-Read" with a "Plug" call by the Safety
   f. "Split-6" defense
   g. "Split" defense with a "Strong" adjustment
2. Sealing the Middle Area. Use:
   a. "Split/Tackles Pinch"
   b. "Split/Backers Fire"
   c. "Split/Tackles In"
   d. "Split/Tackles In, Backers Fire"
   e. "Split-Slant (Liz or Rip)"
   f. "Split-Slant/Backers Fire"
   g. "Split/Tackles In, Sam and Rover In Back"
3. Cutting Off the Outside Plays.
   a. Stopping the Quick Sweeps.
      1) To the Strongside. Use:
         a) "Split-Read"
         b) "Split-Go/Sam In"
         c) "Split-Read/Strong End Zip"
      2) To the Weakside. Use:
         a) "Split-Read"
         b) "Split-Go"
   b. Stopping the Power Sweeps.
      1) To the Strongside. Use:
         a) "Split-Go"
         b) "Split-Go/Sam In"
         c) "Split-Shoot" (vs. Pulling Guards)
         d) "Split/Backers Fire on Flow" (vs. Pulling Linemen)
      2) To the Weakside. Use:
         a) "Split-Go"
         b) "Split-Shoot"
         c) "Split/Backers Fire on Flow"
         d) "Split-Read/Rover Zip"
   c. Stopping the Options.
      1) To the Strongside. Use:
         a) "Split-Go"
         b) "Split-Read/Sam In"
         c) "Split-Read/Sam Stack" (In and Out Calls)

        d) "Split-Read/Sam In Back"

    2) To the Weakside. Use:

        a) "Split-Go"

        b) "Split-Read/Rover Out"

        c) "Split-Read/Rover In"

4. Against the Drop Back Pass.

  a. Attacking the Quarterback:

    1) If the quarterback stays in the Pocket, use a 15-Dog (Ends), 26-Dog (Sam and Rover), or a blitz stunt. Pressure inside with fires, fire-x, or slant fire stunts.

    2) If the quarterback is a scrambler, use a 34-Dog (Backers) or a 26-Dog (Sam and Rover). Apply pressure from the outside and on the corners.

5. Against the Sprint Out Pass.

  a. The Pull-Up Pass: Use regular "Go" and "Shoot' techniques.

  b. The Wide Sprint Out: Use "Go," "Shoot," 34-Dog (Backers), or "Backers Fire on Flow."

6. Attacking the Pass Protection (Drop Back Pass):

  a. Attacking the Backs.

    1) When both backs are poor blockers: Use 34-Dog (Backers) and let Rover, Sam, and the ends attack the protection from the corners.

C.P.: Put in tackles at the end positions and let them run over the backs.

    2) When the strongside back is a poor blocker and the weakside back a good blocker: Use a 36-Dog (Mike and Rover).

    3) When the weakside back is a poor blocker and the strongside back is a good blocker: Use a 24-Dog (Sam and Willie).

  b. Attacking the Line Protection.

    1) When the backs are good blockers, but seldom release into routes, and the quarterback is not a scrambler: Use 15-Dog (Ends), 26-Dog (Sam and Rover), Fires, Fire-X, and Slant Fires. Apply pressure inside from tackle to tackle.

    2) Against Cup Protection: Use Slant Fires, Fire and Fire-X with the Dogs.

    3) Attacking Turn-Out Protection: Use 34-Dog (Backers) or Fires.

7. Combating Special Pass Plays.

  a. Attacking the Deep Passes: Use Fire-X and Slant Fires with the 26-Dog (Sam and Rover) or a 15-Dog (Ends).

  b. Against a team that releases the backs into flare routes: Use 26-Dog (Sam and Rover) or 15-Dog (Ends) if the ends are fast enough to cover the backs.

  c. Against a team that releases backs quick over the middle: Use

34-Dog (Backers) or a 26-Dog (Sam and Rover). If they swing outside of the tackles to reach the middle area, use the 26-Dog (Sam and Rover). Here again the type of personnel will be an important factor to consider. If the offense uses check-through routes or turn-out pass protection blocking to get the backs into position over the middle area, go with the 34-Dog (Backers).

    d. Against a team that releases backs into the flats: Use a 26-Dog (Sam and Rover) or a 15-Dog (Ends), providing the ends are fast enough.

  8. Countering Screens and Draws.

    a. Against Screens.

      1) Against Outside Screens: Use a 26-Dog (Sam and Rover) or a 15-Dog (Ends) depending on personnel limitations. A lot depends on the backfield set; work the dogs accordingly.

      2) Against Inside Screens: Use a 34-Dog (Backers), 24-Dog (Sam and Willie) or a 36-Dog (Mike and Rover).

    b. Against Draws: Use 34-Dog (Backers). Again this depends on the backfield set.

    c. Against Screen and Draw Combinations: Some teams use a certain back to draw to and the other back to screen to. When this happens, adjust the dogs and blitzes accordingly.

      Use a 24-Dog (Sam and Willie), a 36-Dog (Mike and Rover), or a 34-Dog (Backers) depending on the backfield set.

  9. Using Field Position.

    Lateral and vertical field position plays an important part in the selection and the use of the Dog and Blitz stunts. Adjust the Dogs and Blitzes so that the widespread of the field, the short side of the field, the long end of the field, and the short end of the field are used to the maximum.

  10. Against a Tailored or a Semi-Split End.

    Use the "You," "Me" and "Out" stunt. Principles are the same as before. When the offensive end splits to a point he can no longer block down on the defensive end the Sam backer can give a "You" call and support inside of the end on runs. The end now contains.

C. Overall Organizational Outline of the Defensive Battery.

  Since organization is one of the major keys to success in football, it is imperative that the entire defensive system be broken down and categorized into specific groupings. Below you will find such an outline. The specific listing of defenses and stunts under each category may or may not meet your specific needs or philosophy; however, the basic outline for organizing the defensive battery is sound and adaptable to any defensive system at any level.

1. Defenses and Defensive Stunts for Medium Yardage Situations.

a. *Basic*
1) Go
2) Read
3) Shoot

b. *Mixers*
1) Under
2) Over
3) Tackles In and Out
4) Stacks
5) Slants

c. *Pressing*
1) Shoot
2) Fire Stunts
3) If deep in their territory—use Dogs and Blitzes

2. Defenses and Defensive Stunts for Long Yardage Situations.

a. *Basic*
1) Conservative: use Read
2) If they do not release backs into routes, use Go and Fire Stunts.
3) If a sprint out team—use Go or Shoot Techniques

b. *Defend*
1) Read
2) Pro
3) Slam, Hammer and Freeze stunts.

c. *Pressing*
1) Rarely send backs out—use 15-Dog (Ends)
2) Send backs out—use 34-Dog (Backers) or 26-Dog (Sam and Rover)
3) Like draws—use 34-Dog (Backers)
4) Like screens—use 15-Dog (Ends) or 34-Dog (Backers)
5) Like Drop-back pass—use 34-Dog (Ends)
6) Sprint out—use 34-Dog (Backers)
7) Blitzes
8) Blasts

3. Defenses and Defensive Stunts for Short Yardage Situations.

a. *Basic*
1) Go
2) Fire Stunts

b. *Mixers*
1) 70 Mike Gap
2) Tackles In and Out Fires
3) Pinches
4) Stacks

c. *Pressing*
1) Use Dog Stunts
2) Use Blitz Stunts
3) All Ins
4) Blasts

4. Defenses and Defensive Stunts for Pass Rushing Situations.

a. *Drop Back Passes*
1) Go
2) Tackles In and Out Fires
3) Fire and Fire-X Stunts
4) In and In Back Stunts

b. *Sprints*
1) Go
2) Shoot
3) Fire on Flow

c. *Special*
1) Dogs
2) Blitzes

5. Defenses and Defensive Stunts for Pass Defending Situations.

a. *The Long Pass*
1) Read
2) Pro
3) Dogs

b. *The Short Pass*
1) Hammer
2) Slam
3) Freeze

c. For specific routes see Hammer, Slam, Freeze and You-Me principle under Pass Coverages.

d. The Prevent Situation. Use loose alignments such as:
1) Split Loose
2) Pro Loose

D. Special Coaching Points, Problems and Remedies.

1. Containment.

In the split alignment the defensive ends must contain all outside plays, especially when the secondary is hooked up in man-to-man coverage. If the outside receivers threaten cross field or deep, the halfbacks will be down the field and unavailable for quick run support on a sprint out or quarterback scramble.

Therefore, the ends must work hard on containment; and the entire team must be aware of the need for quick pursuit and making the "Run, Run" call which will release the halfbacks from their pass responsibilities.

When the secondary defenders hear the "Run, Run" call, they can forget the receivers and support against the run as quickly as possible.

2. Covering for Stunters. When the inside linebackers are stunting, the tackles should use "read" techniques. When the inside linebackers and the tackles are involved in stunts, the ends should use "read" techniques. When one inside linebacker and one tackle are involved in a stunt, the other inside linebacker and tackle should use "read" techniques. When the outside linebackers are stunting, the inside linebackers usually use "read" techniques covering for them. In "Team" stunts all reading techniques are discarded.

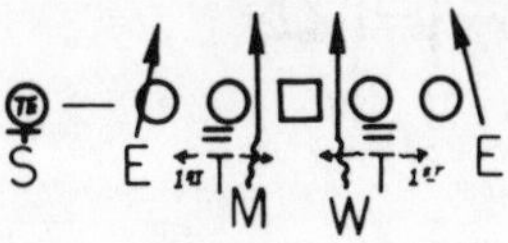

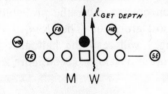

a) *"Backers Fire" Stunt*

b) *"Tackles Out Fire" Stunt*

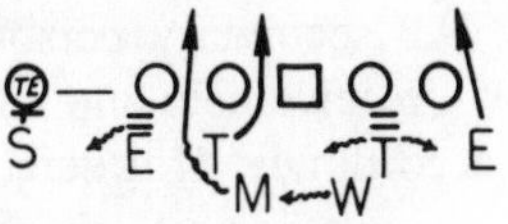

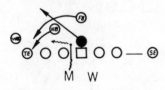

c) *"Mike deal" Stunt*

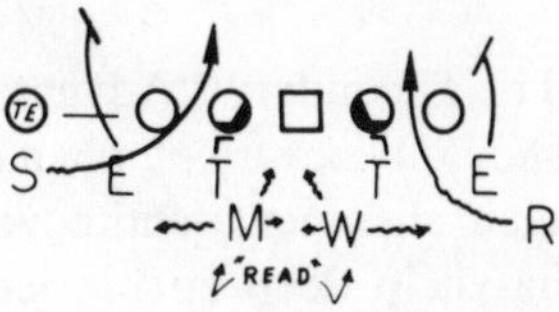

d) *Sam and Rover "Out" Stunt*

Figure 267a, b, c and d Various "Read" Techniques used to cover for stunters.

3. Linebacker Variable Penetration Techniques. All stunters should keep in mind the down, the distance, the situation, and the type of offense the opponents use; for this will influence the type of stunt charge to be used. For example, against a drop-back passing team in a long yardage situation a fire stunt should be of the deep penetrating type with no worry of lateral adjustment. The same stunt against a power sweep team in a running situation should be altered in some respects because lateral adjustment after the initial stunt move is highly desirable. See Figures 268 a, b, c, d, e, and f.

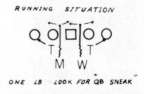

a) *In passing situation*

b) *In running situations*

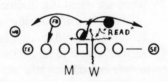

c) *vs. sprint out team*

d) *Look for QB sneak-short yardage and running situations*

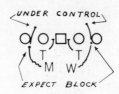

UNDER CONTROL

EXPECT BLOCK

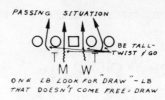

PASSING SITUATION

BE TALL—
TWIST / GO

ONE LB LOOK FOR "DRAW" — LB
THAT DOESN'T COME FREE = DRAW

e) Expect, position, and meet blocks with correct form

f) Look for draw-passing situations

Figure 268a, b, c, d, e, & f Variation in stunt charges

4. The Secondary "Advantage" Techniques. All secondary personnel should be aware of when and where they will receive help and adjust their alignments and coverage techniques accordingly. If a defender has help deep and inside, he can afford to give himself the "advantage" by aligning slightly more to the outside which will aid in covering the outside routes. However, this is not true of all coverages, so alignments must be adjusted accordingly by applying the common sense rule.

KNOW WHERE "MIKE" GOES

UNDERNEATH HELP

DEEP MIDDLE HELP

Figure 269 Gold/Free Man with Help Locations

5. The Secondary's "Keys and Probability" Rule. By reading the proper key the offense will give away its intentions. For example, when the weakside halfback takes an outside route the probability of the split end running a curl or post are great. Therefore, if the Rover (in Gold/Free Man Coverage) will read the halfback, he should have a jump on the route before it develops. (See Figure 270 a, b, c and d.)

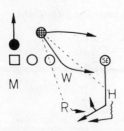

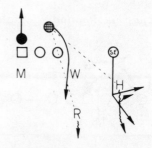

a) Halfback outside release—Curl and Post

b) Halfback inside release—Sideline and Flag

210

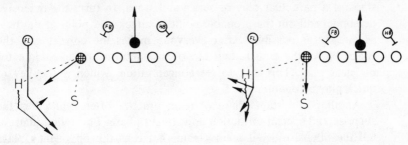

*c) Tight end takes outside route
—Curl and Post*

*d) Tight end releases straight—
Sideline and Flag*

Figure 270a, b, c, and d Complementary Patterns

6. The Secondary's "Receiver Delay or Block" Rules. If the tight end delays, the Sam backer will hold and pick up the tight end man-for-man (exception: when back flares wide, Sam picks up the back and Mike picks up the delayed tight end). This in turn frees the strong safety who can now drift deep and help the strong side defensive halfback on the post route.

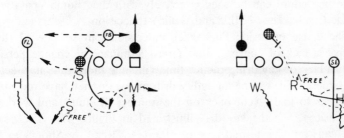

*a) Tight End Delays—Safety
Free to Play Post Route*

*b) Weak Back Blocks—Rover
Moves Across Face of Split End*

Figure 271a and b When Receivers Delay or Block

7. Emphasize Play Recognition and Third Down Situations During Team Practice Periods.

The defensive coach should divide the team practice period into various phases, placing emphasis on the problem areas. Some important phases that should be included in team periods during the week are: concentrated play recognition, short yardage situations, long yardage situations, third down clutch situations, surprise and special formation adjustments, and goal line stands (the kicking period should be separate, but not always at the end of practice).

If quick play recognition is a problem, use a 2- or 3-step read drill. In this drill the offensive scout team executes two or three steps of a particular play or series and stops. In turn, the defensive personnel call out the probable point of attack and point at the hole as quickly as possible. After everyone makes the correct call, the coach blows the whistle and the offense returns to the huddle for the next play. This drill forces concentration, which is the key to quick play recognition.

Another important phase of team practice often omitted is the surprise and special formation adjustment phase. For added interest, tell the offensive scout team (team that runs the opponent's plays against the defensive unit) that on a given signal (from defensive coach) they can sprint to the line of scrimmage, line up anywhere from sideline to sideline; includes all personnel), and do anything they want. If they score, let them do fewer wind sprints, or let them out of sprints completely to devise something for the next day's practice. Let the scout team quarterback be the coach.

If the scout team is properly motivated, you will be surprised at what they will devise and how much fun they will have in doing it.

When the team period begins to drag (as all team periods do at some time or other), give the signal and wake up the defense. This same procedure can be used effectively with the "bomb" pass.

8. Inside Linebackers' (Mike and Willie) Indecision.

The cause of inside linebacker indecision can be one of three things: a lack of concentration (must stimulate or change personnel), a lack of key drill practice time (include more time in practice on the key drill; can be an agility drill also), or they have too many decisions to make (cut back on the number of stunts and work on the basics). See the key drill illustrated in Figure 272. The coach (C) calls out the desired type of play (Go, Read, or Shoot) or the stunt (also give a call of "running situation" or "passing situation." Refer to "Linebacker variable penetration techniques" in this section) and then simulate the "keys" possible action. Strive for quick reads and proper positioning. As the linebackers become more efficient at this drill, add small obstacles in their lanes for agility work or add a backfield to complicate their reads. See Figure 272 a, b, and c.

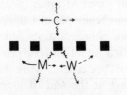

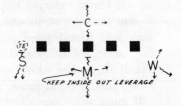

a) Split Defense—Key drill   *b) Pro Defense—Key drill*

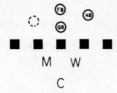

c) Backfield Key Drill

Figure 272a, b, and c The Linebacker Key Drill

GLOSSARY OF TERMS
USED IN THIS BOOK

A. Defensive Personnel.
  1. Linebackers:
     SAM: The strongside linebacker. Also known as Number "2."
     MIKE: The strongside inside linebacker. Also known as Number "3."
     WILLIE: The weakside inside linebacker. Also known as Number "4."
     ROVER: The weakside linebacker. Also known as Number "6."
  2. Ends:
     LEFT END: The defensive end on the left side of the formation. Also known as Number "1."
     RIGHT END: The defensive end on the right side of the formation. Also known as Number "5."
  3. Tackles:
     LEFT TACKLE: The first down lineman on the left side of the center.
     RIGHT TACKLE: The first down lineman on the right side of the center.
  4. Secondary:
     FOX: The defensive safety.
     HOUNDS: The defensive halfbacks.
B. Alignments.
  STACKED: A backer aligned directly behind a defensive lineman.
  PRO: An adjustment moving the tackles to a head-up position on the guards and Willie to an outsider linebacker position. Used as an automatic and a basic defense.

LOOSE: A position 2-2½ yards off the line of scrimmage and in a 2-point linebacker type stance.

DOWN: A four point position on the line of scrimmage. A position used by the Sam linebacker in short yardage situations.

SWITCH: Exchange of positions or assignments between two players, usually the Sam linebacker and the onside defensive end.

SLOT: Special adjustment to a slot alignment.

RED: A secondary alignment (3 deep with Rover on the strong side of the formation).

BLUE: A secondary alignment (3 deep with Rover on the split end side of the formation).

GOLD: A secondary alignment (4 deep with Rover at the free safety position).

C. Types of Charges (Tackles and Inside Linebackers).

"Go": An all-out attack directed at the offensive personnel by the defensive tackles and the inside linebackers (Mike and Willie).

"Read": A non-penetrating type of play by the tackles and inside linebackers (Mike and Willie).

"Shoot": The inside linebacker (Mike or Willie) on the side away from flow shoots through the line toward flow and attempts to catch the ball carrier from behind. The other linebacker uses read techniques.

D. Stunts.

1. Up Front Stunts.

a. Individual stunts (One man stunts):

"ZIP": A one-man stunt involving Sam, Rover, the end, or a secondary man. (A crashing type charge across the line of scrimmage.)

"FIRE": An inside linebacker (Mike or Willie) stunt. Can be one or both linebackers stunting.

b. Unit stunts (Two-man stunts):

"IN": A two-man stunt involving Sam and the end, Rover and the end or the tackles.

"OUT": A two-man stunt involving the tackles, Rover and the end, or Sam and the end after a switch.

"IN BACK": A two-man stunt between Sam and the onside end.

"X": A crossing action between two defensive men (backers, tackles and ends).

"PINCH": A squeezing charge by the tackles, Sam and the end, or Rover and the end.

"DEAL": A stunt between an inside linebacker and the onside tackle.

"SLANT": An angle charge by the tackles (can be left or right).

"BACKERS FIRE": Both inside linebackers firing (Mike and Willie).

c. Group stunts (Four-man stunts):

"BLAST": A four-man, all-out rush on one side of the center or the other (right or left).

d. Team stunts (More than four defenders stunting):

"DOG": In this book, Dog is referred to as an all-out, six-man rush against the pass and run.

"BLITZ": In this book, Blitz is referred to as an all-out, seven-man rush against the pass and run.

"ALL": Everyone is involved in the stunt called (All In, All Pinch, All Blitz, etc.)

E. Secondary Stunts.

1. Individual Stunts.

"ZIP": If a secondary man's name is added to a "Zip" call, he will stunt across the line of scrimmage and through the hole indicated.

2. Unit and Group Stunts.

"HAMMER": The halfback attacks the outside receiver and applies pressure outside In (bump-and-go).

"SLAM": The safety or Rover (or both) attacks the outside receiver and applies pressure inside Out (bump-and-go).

"HEADS": An alignment on the line of scrimmage and head-on, inside shoulder or outside shoulder of a receiver.

"CUT": A side-body block used to cut a receiver to the ground as he attempts to leave the line of scrimmage or two or three yards down the field.

"FREEZE": A maneuver used to attack a receiver four yards down the field.

"UNDER": Playing between the line of scrimmage and the receiver for the interception (can be under and outside or under and inside). Used in special coverages.

"OVER": Playing over the top of a receiver (can be over and inside or over and outside). Used in special coverages.

3. Secondary Coverages.

BLUE ROLL: A combination zone and man coverage used against tight formations.

BLUE MAN: Straight man coverage without a free safety.

NUMBERS: Straight man coverage with variable man coverage underneath.

BLUE/CHECK-3: Straight three deep zone coverage with outside linebackers zoning the flats.

BLUE/ZONE COVER-1: A rotating zone on play action away from the Rover.

BLUE/ZONE COVER-2: A rotating zone on drop back and action away from the Rover.

GOLD/FREE MAN: Straight man coverage with a free safety to help on the deep inside routes.

BLUE/SEMI ROLL: Partial rotations on drop back and action toward a slot. Used against slot formation.

BLUE/SINGLE MAN: Safety rolls both ways with flow; on side halfback attacks onside receiver and the backside halfback picks up his receiver man-to-man.

GOLD/STRONG ZONE: A four-deep rotating zone to the strong side of the offensive formation.

GOLD/WEAK ZONE: A four-deep rotating zone to the weak side of the offensive formation.

    4. Team Stunt Coverages.

"DOGS": Secondary uses blue-man coverage.

"BLITZES": Secondary uses blue-man coverage.

F. Special Calls.

    1. Front Calls:

"MOVE": A huddle call indicating a quick shift from one defensive alignment to another on a specific key.

"NOW": A command used at the line of scrimmage by the Mike backer calling for a shift of the defense to another alignment.

    2. Calls Between the Backers and Tackles:

"GAP": Shifts tackle to gap.

"CENTER": Shifts tackle to position on center.

"SLOT": Shifts tackle to head-on position over guard.

"CHECK PRO": Tackles move to head-on position over guards.

"RIP": An automatic call used at the line of scrimmage meaning "right."

"LIZ": An automatic call used at the line of scrimmage meaning "left."

    3. Calls Between the Rover and Backers:

"GONE": Informs Willie that he will have the first back out on his side if a pass develops.

"ONE": Informs Willie he will pick up the first back out on his side (if he releases) if flow is away from him.

"TWO": Informs Willie he has the first back out on his side (if he releases) on flow away and drop-back action.

    4. Calls in the Secondary:

"YOU": A call from the safety to the halfback; halfback rolls to flat and the safety covers the deep outside 1/3 of the field.

"ME": A call from the safety to the halfback; safety rolls to flat and the halfback covers the deep outside 1/3 of the field.

"Crack": Alerts end or Rover of the crack back block by a split end or flanker.

"CHECK-3": Secondary plays three deep zones regardless of flow.

"CHECK-MAN": Secondary coverage reverts to basic man-to-man coverage.

5. Calls Between the Outside Backers (Sam and Rover) and Ends:

"YOU": The end contains and the outside linebacker has inside fill vs. runs.

"ME": The end has inside responsibilities against runs and the outside linebacker has outside contain.

"SWITCH": The end plays on the outside shoulder of the tackle and the backer aligns in the contain position.

"OUT": The end stunts outside and contains while Sam or Rover stunts inside to fill the off-tackle area.

"GONE": This call informs the defensive end on the split end side of the formation that Rover or Sam is gone and will not be able to help with immediate support inside or outside of him.

G. General Terms.

1. DEFENSE:

AUTOMATICS: An audible call used at the line of scrimmage to give directions or change assignments.

CONTAIN: Keeping the ball inside of position held.

DEFENSIVE BATTERY: A number of defenses chosen for a particular season or game.

FOCAL POINT: A spot or small area on which defenders' eyes are fixed.

FORMATION DEFENSE: Defense designed to cope with possibilities presented by a particular offensive formation.

FOOTBALL POSITION: A crouched position from which most football fundamentals are executed.

KEY: Offensive man or men to watch to gain a step on the offense.

PERSONNEL DEFENSE: Defense designed to cope with key personnel.

PRO: The alternate defensive alignment discussed in this book (a Pro type 4-3 alignment).

PURSUIT ANGLE: The shortest angle to reach the ball carrier before he scores.

STANCE: Alignment of feet and body.

SPLIT: The basic defense discussed in this book.

TAP: A technique used by a linebacker to adjust the lateral position of a down lineman on the line of scrimmage (left or right.)

TECHNIQUE: A systematic method used in performing an assignment.

TENDENCY: A predictable pattern.

TENDENCY DEFENSE: A defense specially designed to cope with the plays used by the opponents from a particular alignment in certain situations.

TRAIL: A route behind the line of scrimmage used to follow the ball carrier.

2. Offense:

COUNTER: Ball carrier running opposite of flow.

DOUBLE TEAM: Two offensive blockers vs. one defender.

FLOW: Direction in which most of the offensive backs move.

INFLUENCE BLOCK: An offensive lineman's technique used to set up a defensive man playing on him for trap block.

LEAD BLOCK: Back blocking through hole on a linebacker.

NEAR BACK: The back nearest side being discussed.

OFF SIDE: Side of formation away from the point of attack.

ON SIDE: Side of formation to which the point of attack is directed.

REMAINING BACKS: Backs that remain in the backfield in a formation involving a flanker.

STRONGBACK: Back located on the strong side of the formation.

STRONG SIDE: The side of the formation where the most players are aligned.

THE TWO RECEIVER SIDE: Side of the formation that has two quick receivers (Wing, Slot, or Flanker).

WEAKBACK: Back located on the weak side of the formation.

WEAK SIDE: The side of the formation where the fewest players are aligned.

INDEX

A

Advantages of Split defense, 19, 24
Alignments, term, 214–215
"All," term, 216
Attacking techniques and stunts, 173–182
   (see also Stunts and attacking techniques)
Automatics, term, 218

B

Backer Unit, 20
"Backers Fire," term, 216
"Ball, ball" call, 149
Belly, 29
"Blast," term, 216
"Blitz," term, 216, 217
Blocking problems, creating, 15–19
Blue, term, 215
Blue/Check-3, term, 216
Blue Man, term, 216
Blue Roll, term, 216
Blue/Semi Roll, term, 217
Blue/Single Man, term, 217
Blue/Zone Cover-1, term, 216
Blue/Zone Cover-2, term, 217
"Box" call, 31
"Bump-and-Go," 174–175

C

"Center," term, 217
Charges, term, 215
"Check-Man," term, 218

"Check Pro," term, 217
"Check-Strong," 191
"Check-3," term, 218
Contain, term, 218
Counter, term, 219
Coverage:
  secondary pass, 135–152
    (see also Pass coverage, secondary)
  secondary team, 155–171
    (see also Team coverage, secondary)
"Crack," term, 218
"Curl" call, 147, 163
"Cut," term, 216

D

"D" position, 50, 56
"Deal," term, 215
"Deep" call, 147
Defenses, basic, 22–23
Defensive battery, term, 218
Defensive personnel, 214
Defensive system:
  attacking pass protection, 205
  coaching points, problems, remedies, 208–213
  combating special pass plays, 205–206
  containment, 208
  covering for stunters, 208–209
  defensive strategy, 201–206
  inside linebackers' indecision, 212
  linebacker variable penetration techniques, 209
  overall organizational outline, 206–208
  play recognition, 211–212

Defensive system (*cont.*)
secondary "advantage" techniques, 210
secondary's "Keys and Probability"
rule, 210–211
secondary's "Receiver Delay or Block"
rules, 211
Split-Pro Huddle Alignment, 199–200
huddle, 199–200
huddle procedure, 200
post huddle alignment, 200
third down situations, 211–212
using field position, 206
Development of Split Pro, 13–24
(*see also* Evolution)
Dive, 29
"Dog," term, 216
"Dogs," term, 217
Double team, term, 219
Down, term, 215

E

"Easy" call, 152
Ends:
calls, 27–28, 31, 45
"Box," 31
"Gone," 28
"Head," 45
"Me," 27
"No call," 28
"You," 27
concept, 27
focal point, 28
initial move, 29
keys and techniques, 29–30
Belly or Lead, 29
Dive and Option, 29
Flow Away, 30
Hook, 29
Kick Out, 29
Pass Protects, 29
Pitch and Quick Outside Plays, 29–30
"Loose" call, 31
"Pro" defense alignment, 31–33
qualifications, 27
responsibilities, 27
rushing the passer, 33–35
coaching points, 35
ends' pass rush techniques, 33–35
general concept, 33
Split rules, 30
stance, 28
stunts, 35–46
group, 42
individual, 35–36
listed by category, 46
team, 43–45

unit, 36–42
"Switch" call, 30–31
term, 214
Evolution:
advantages of Split defense, 24
aiding the secondary, 15
backers, 15
background, 14–15
basic defenses, 22–23
blocking confusion for running game, 13
blocking problems created, 15–19
college and professional film study, 13
combination of ideas, 13
designation and manipulation of units
and stunts, 20–21
developing the system, 19–23
Eagle defense, 13, 14
ends, 15
5-4 monster defense, 13, 14
flip-flopping personnel, 21
important aspects of Split Defense, 19
mixture easily obtained, 13
multi-stunting 4-4, 13
Neale, Greasy, 13, 14
outgrowth, 13
overloading, 13
personnel, identification, 19–20
"Pro" part of defense, 22
"Pro," term, 14
Pro type 4-3, 13
separate units, 19
sessions with coaches, 17
"Split" and "Pro" defenses, 13
split principle, 14
Split-6 defense, 13, 14
"Split," term, 14
start of system, 14–22
summary, 23–24
trial and error, 13
two basic starting alignments, 13
ultimate in pass coverage, 13
wide tackle-6 defense, 13, 14

F

F, 20
"50" Defense, 122, 132
"Fire," term, 215
Flip-flopping personnel, 21
Flow, term, 219
Flow Away, 30
Focal point, term, 218
Football position, term, 218
"Force" position, 86
Formation defense, term, 218
Fox, term, 214
"Freeze," term, 216

G

"Gap," term, 217
"Go," term, 215
Gold, term, 215
Gold/Free Man, term, 217
Gold/Strong Zone, term, 217
Gold/Weak Zone, term, 217
"Gone," term, 217, 218

H

H, 20, 50, 128
"Hammer," term, 216
"Heads," term, 216
"Heads-Call," 55
"Hitch," 163
Hook, 29
Hounds, term, 214

I

"I" position, 50
"In Back," term, 215
"In," term, 215
Influence block, term, 219
Inside linebacker:
    alignments, 72
    basic types of play, 72–77
    coaching points, 78
    controlling excessive line splits, 79
    general concept, 71
    "Go" techniques, 72–73
    keys, 72
    pass coverage-split defense, 79–84
        adjusting to field position, 82
        covering backs out, 82
        pass keys and special tips, 82–83
        reactions to drop-back pass, 79–81
    "Pro" defense alignments, 84–88
    "Shoot" techniques, 77
    special calls, 83
        "Check-Pro," 84
        "Gone," 83
        "One," 83
        "Two," 84
    "Split Read" techniques, 76
    "Split-Shoot" techniques, 76–77
    stance, 72
    stunts and stunting techniques, 88–104
        "All" Calls, 99–100
        "Backers Fire," 89
        "Backers Fire on Flow," 90
        "Backers Fire-X," 90
        "Blast," 94–95
        "Blitz," 99
        "Dog" and "Blitz" Principles, 95–99
        general concept, 88
        individual, 88–89

list, 104
"Mike Deal," 91
Mike "Fire," 88
"Pro-Backers Fire," 101
"Pro-Backers Fire-X," 101
"Pro-Tackles In," 100
"Pro-Tackles In—Fire on Flow,"
    101
"Pro-Tackles Pinch," 101
"Pro-Tackles Slant," 100
"Pro-Tackles Slant—Backers Fire,"
    101
"Tackles In—Backers Read or Fire,"
    91
"Tackles In—Fire on Flow," 92
"Tackles In—Mike or Willie Fire,"
    92
"Tackles Out," 100
"Tackles Out—Backers Read or
    Fire," 93
"Tackles Out—Shoot," 93
"Tackles Slant (Liz or Rip)—Back-
    ers Read or Fire," 94
    unit, 89–91
"Willie Deal," 91
Willie "Fire," 89
"Willie Gap-Fire," 90
"Tackles Go—Backers Read," 77
"Tackles Read—Backers Go," 77
techniques, 72–79
"I've Got Him," call, 152

K

Key, term, 218
Kick Out, 29

L

"L" position, 50, 55
LE, 20
Lead, 29
Lead block, term, 219
Linebackers, term, 214
"Liz," term, 217
Look-In Pass, 132, 163
Loose, term, 215
LT, 20

M

M, 20
"Man" call, 138–143
"Me," term, 217, 218
Mike, term, 214
Mike and Willie, 71–104
    (see also Inside linebacker)
"Move," term, 217

N

Neale, Greasy, 13
Near back, term, 219
"No call," 28, 126
Nose Defense, 132, 190
"Now," term, 217
Numbers, term, 216

O

"O" position, 50, 56
Off side, term, 219
"OH" defense, 189
On side, term, 219
"One," term, 217
"Out or Sideline" pass, 163
"Out," term, 215, 218
Outside linebacker stunts, 62–67
"Over," term, 216

P

Pass coverage, secondary:
  alignments (color calls), 137–138
  "ball, ball," 149
  "Blue," 137
  calls, 138–152
  "Check-Man" call, 152
  "Check-3" call, 152
  combination, 144
  "Crack" call, 149, 152
  "Curl" call, 147
  "Deep" call, 147
  "Easy" call, 152
  general concept, 135–136
  "Gold," 138
  huddle, 136–137
  individual position play, 148–152
  "I've Got Him," call, 152
  "Man" call, 138–143
  "Plug" call, 152
  "Red," 137
  "run, run" call, 150
  secondary and underneath, 144–148
  "Switch" call, 152
  "You or Me" calls, 152
  "Zone" call, 143–144
Personnel defense, term, 218
Personnel, identification, 19–20
"Pinch," term, 215
"Plug" call, 66, 152
"Post," 163
Principle, 14
Pro, term, 214, 218
"Pro/Blue, Check-3," 168
"Pro/Blue Heads, Check 3," 169
"Pro/Gold, Free Man," 168–169
"Pro/Gold, Strong Zone," 167

"Pro/Gold, Weak Zone," 167
"Pro" part of defense, 13, 22
"Pro-Willie Stack," 86
Pursuit angle, term, 218

Q

"Quick Out," 163

R

R, 20
RE, 20
"Read," term, 215
Red, term, 215
Remaining backs, term, 219
"Rip," term, 217
Rover:
  alignments, 126–129
  calls, 125–126
  "50" Defense, 132
  general concepts, 125
  pass coverage, 132
  pass keys, 132
  "Pro" Defense, 131–132
  Seventy and Nose Defenses, 132
  stunts, 129–132
    general concept, 129
    individual, 129
    list, 132
    team, 130–131
    unit, 129–130
  term, 214
  Under and Over Defenses, 132
Rover Unit, 20
RT, 20
"Run/run" call, 150

S

S, 20, 50
Sam, term, 214
Sam Unit, 20
"Sam" position:
  adjustments, 56
  alignment, rules, 50
  alternate alignments, 62
  basic techniques and variations, 51–56
  "basic" pass coverage techniques, 56–59
  call, 66
  covering motion, 61–62
  "D" technique, 56
  general concept, 49–50
  "Heads-Call," 55
  "I" technique, 51–54
    alignment, 51
    focal point, 51
    general rule, 51

"Sam" position (*cont.*)
  "I" technique (*cont.*)
    initial movement, 51
    purpose, 51
    responsibilities, 52–54
    stance, 51
  "L" technique, 55
  "O" technique, 56
  outside linebacker stunts, 62–67
    group, 64
    individual, 62
    list, 67
    team, 65–66
    unit, 63–64
  "Plug" call, 66
  possible playing positions, 50
  Sam Switch vs. Nasty End Split, 54
  split rules, 54
  straight "zone" pass coverage, 60–61
  "switch" position split rules, 54–55
Secondary:
  pass coverage, 135–152
    (*see also* Pass coverage, secondary)
  stunts and attacking techniques, 173–
    182
    (*see also* Stunts and attacking techniques)
  team coverages, 155–171
    (*see also* Team coverage, secondary)
  term, 214
"Semi-Roll," 163–165
"70" Defense, 121–122, 132, 190
"Shoot," term, 215
"Single-Man," 165–167
"Slam," term, 216
"Slant," term, 215
"Slot," term, 215, 217
"Split" part of defense, 13
Split-Pro, evolution, 13–24
  (*see also* Evolution)
Split, term, 218
Stacked, term, 214
Stance, term, 218
Strong side, term, 219
Strongback, term, 219
Strongside linebacker techniques, 49–67
  (*see also* "Sam" position)
Stunts and attacking techniques:
  "Bump-and-Go," 174–175
  "Cut," 176
  defending secondary stunts, 178–182
  defending team stunts, 174
  "Freeze," 176–177
  general concept, 173
  "Hammer," 175–176
  "Heads," 177
  pressure team stunts, 174
  secondary attacking techniques, 174–
    177

secondary team stunts, 174
"Slam," 175
unit stunts, 173–174
"Switch," term, 215, 218

                    T

Tackle techniques:
  "Butt and Go," 115
  "Check Pro," 113
  defensive tackle play, 108–114
  "Dog and Blitz" pass charges, 114
  "Fake and Club," 115
  "50" Defense, 122
  general concept, 107
  "Hand Blow and Club," 115
  "Nose Charge," 114
  "Outside Shoulder Drive," 115
  "Pinch," 113
  "Pro" Defense, 121
  rushing the passer, 115–117
    general concept, 115
    keys, 116–117
    pass rushing techniques, 115–116
  "70" Defense, 121–122
  "Shoot" techniques, 112–113
  special calls, 114–115
  "Spin," 115
  split "go," 112
  split "read," 108–111
    alignment, 108
    focal point, 108
    movement, 108–109
    "read" techniques, 109–111
    stance, 108
  stunts, 117–121
    individual, 117
    Pro-defense, 120
    team, 119–120
    unit and group, 118–119
  "Tight" Defense, 122
  "Trap," 113
Tackle Unit, 20
"Tackles In Fire," 191
Tap, term, 218
Team coverage, secondary:
  "Blue Check-3," 159
  "Blue Man," 157–158
  "Blue Roll," 156
  "Blue-Zone, Cover 1," 159–160
  "Blue-Zone, Cover-2," 161–163
  covering motion, 169–171
  general concept, 155
  "Gold/Free-Man," 163
  "Numbers," 158–159
  "Pro/Blue, Check-3," 168
  "Pro-Blue Heads, Check 3," 168
  Pro-Defense, 167–169
  "Pro/Gold, Free Man," 168–169
  "Pro/Gold, Strong Zone," 167

Team coverage, secondary (*cont.*)
  "Pro/Gold, Weak Zone," 167
  "Semi-Roll," 163–165
  "Single Man," 165–167
  split defense, 156–167
Team defenses:
  automatics, 190–191
    "Check-Pro," 190
    "Check-Strong," 191
    "Gap-Tackle," 191
    "One-Left," 191
    "One-Right," 191
  blitz stunts, 193–194
  defensive alignments, 185–189
  Dog stunts, 191–193
    "15-Dog (Ends)," 192
    rules, 191–192
    "34-Dog," 192
    "36-Dog," 192
    "24-Dog," 193
    "26-Dog," 192
  goal line defense, 197
  list of basic defensive alignments, 186
  mixers, 189
  "OH," 189
  pass defend, 194–197
    concept, 194
    prevent defenses, 196–197
    solid defend defenses, 195
    stunting defend, 195–196
  pass rushes, 191
  pressure team stunts, 191–194
  "Pro," 187–188
  short yardage defenses, 190
  "Split," 185
  Split-6, 188
  "Tight," 188
  "Wide," 189
Technique, term, 218

Tendency, term, 219
Tendency defense, term, 219
"Tight" Defense, 122
Trail, term, 219
"Two," term, 217
Two Receiver Side, term, 219

U

"Under," term, 216

W

W, 20, 50, 128
Weak outside linebacker techniques, 125–133
  (*see also* Rover)
Weak side, term, 219
Weakback, term, 219
"Wide" defense, 189
Willie, term, 214
"Willie Stack" call, 86

X

"X," 215

Y

"You," 217, 218
"You Close," 85, 128
"You Walk," 85–86

Z

"Zip," 215, 216
"Zone" call, 143–144